Dealing with UNPROFITABLE FOUNDATIONS

Dr. D. K. Olukoya

DEALING WITH THE UNPROFITABLE FOUNDATION

Dr. D. K. Olukoya
MFM Ministries
Lagos, Nigeria.

© 1999
DEALING WITH THE UNPROFITABLE FOUNDATION
Dr. D. K. Olukoya

A publication of
**TRACTS AND PUBLICATIONS GROUP
MOUNTAIN OF FIRE AND MIRACLES MINISTRIES**
13, Olasimbo Street, Off Olumo Road,
(By UNILAG Second Gate), Onike, Iwaya
P.O.Box 2990, Sabo, Yaba, Lagos, Nigeria.
01-868766
Email: mfm@micro.com.ng
mfm@nigol.net.ng
Website: www.mountain-of-fire.com

All rights reserved. No part of this publication may be reproduced, stored in a retrieval system, or be transmitted, in any form, or by any means, mechanically, electronic, photocopying or otherwise without the prior written consent of the publisher. It is protected under the copyright laws.

ISBN: 978-2947-64-4

Typesetting, design and printing at
MFM PRESS
13, Olasimbo Street, Off Olumo Raod,
by Unilag 2nd Gate, Onike,
Yaba, Lagos, Nigeria.

Cover Illustration by: Sis. Shade Olukoya.

TABLE OF CONTENT

PREFACE iv

Chapter One
THE SICK FOUNDATION 1

Chapter Two
PULLING DOWN FOUNDATIONAL JERICHO 11

Chapter Three
EATERS OF FLESH AND DRINKERS OF BLOOD ... 29

Chapter Four
THE POWERS THAT PURSUE 42

Chapter Five
THE UNPROFITABLE COVENANT 58

Chapter Six
TABLE OF THE LORD AND TABLE OF THE DEVIL ... 65

Chapter Seven
THE POWER IN THE BLOOD 73

Chapter Eight
IMMUNITY AGAINST THE OPPRESSORS 89

Chapter Nine
DECLARE WAR ON SATAN'S WAR 102

PREFACE

"The Spirit of the Lord is upon me, because He hath anointed me to preach the gospel to the poor; He hath sent me to heal the broken-hearted, to preach deliverance to the captives, and recovery of sight to the blind, to set at liberty those that are bruised." (Luke 4:18)

This book has been written so that the veil satan has carefully woven over the faces of men would be removed. By the special grace of God given to me in the course of my years of ministering, I have discovered that many, even so called believers do not understand what salvation is all about, not to talk of enjoying it. Salvation includes deliverance for spiritual captives in the spirit.

One of satan's best instruments against believers is ignorance. Another reason this work was put together is to expose the subtle ways through which the devil has contaminated many lives thereby preventing them from realizing the purpose of God for their lives. Finally this book is written by an African who has seen demonic manifestations in diverse forms. Many of the examples given in this book will appear very strange to some people, but by the grace of God, they are all real life encounters I have had with some people one time or another. The purpose of the scripture is not just for you to be able to recite it, rather as apostle Paul said: "For your gospel came not unto you in word only, but also in power, and in the Holy Ghost."

This book is a practical guide for any one with the determination to experience the power in the name of Jesus Christ as the only name given unto man for salvation. Demonic activity is on the increase and will continue to heighten until the coming of our Lord and Saviour Jesus Christ, but you can be free if you wish.

All the chapters in this book have been preached as messages directed by God at our fellowship in the past. Each of these messages was followed by instant manifestation of God's power to break contrary covenants and hitherto unbreakable yokes. You too can experience deliverance in your spirit as you read this book. Prepare yourself for earth shaking testimonies that will take you into new realms of the fullness of salvation.

Chapter One
THE SICK FOUNDATION

Dealing With The Unprofitable Foundation

"And the rain descended, and the floods came, and the winds blew, and beat upon the house; and it fell. And great was the fall of it." (Matthew 7:27)

Most things in life are in values of two, for example, black and white, light and darkness, male and female and lastly good and bad. Buildings that collapse in life are often as a result of a foundational problem. The foundation of any building is very vital and any building with faulty foundation can not be said to be good or alright regardless of the external beauty or magnificence. There is a fact everybody must know: the storms, wind and adversity of life do not discriminate between a good foundation and a sick one. The only difference is that a solid foundation will still stand because of its staying power when the weather becomes harsh. The Psalmist realized early that it is the foundation that makes the difference between success and failure, progress and retrogression, victory and defeat, and all other things are secondary.

"If the foundation be destroyed, what can the righteous do?" (Psalms 11:3)

Many people are going on as if they have sound foundation whereas their foundation has already been destroyed. They do not understand why everything they lay their hands on does not prosper in spite of the fact that all the inputs are there for success. Most seemingly intractable problems are as a result of sick foundation. Solving such problems can be done only by going to the foundation of such a life. *"And about the time of her death the women that stood by her said unto her, fear not; for thou hast born a son, but she answered not, neither did she regard it. And she named the child Ichabod, saying, The glory is departed from Israel because the ark of God had been taken, and because of her father-in-law and her husband."* (I Samuel 4:20-21)

The life of Ichabod would definitely be a harvest of problems. He would hear of success, see people live fulfilled lives, but his life would be a disappointment on all fronts. Ichabod started having problems from the womb. At his birth, his father died. His grandfather also died and most importantly, the symbol of God's glory departed from the land. All these negative circumstances got firmly rooted in his life by the name he was given. Anybody that would help Ichabod would have to take a spiritual journey back to the day he was born. Many people placed the ladder of their lives on the wrong walls only to reach the top and discover serious problems. Some others are building the structures of their lives on contaminated foundation. Yet many more have even completed the building of their lives on polluted foundation.

Our past is gone but not dead, that is why it is often said that our tomorrow is what we make of our today. Many lives are in shambles today not because of the things they are doing now but because of the evil they had done years ago. If your life at present will not be ruled by your past, you must be washed by the blood of the Lamb and soaked in the word of God. You must also receive genuine baptism in the Holy Spirit. Anything short of this will mean that your future will continue to be conditioned by your past. Jesus Christ looked at the Jews and made a deep pronouncement in John 5:45:

"Do not think that I will accuse you to the Father; there is one that accuseth you, even Moses, in whom you trust." The Jews revered Moses and anything anybody said against Moses was regarded as blasphemy.

However, this same people did not understand that the Moses of their past was accusing them before God. How can you be free from this accusation? Only God's divine intervention can salvage this situation, no other power can. If you desire God's intervention, there are some dangerous possessions you must not have:

1. A life without Christ.
2. Talent without godly consecration.
3. Ability to do something without godly character.
4. Zeal without knowledge.
5. Knowledge without wisdom.
6. God's power and authority without godly compassion.
7. Gifts without love. These things must be in their appropriate position in any life that will experience God's deliverance power from a sick foundation.

Most things happening to people now are as a result of events that happened many years ago. Many years ago, when I was a student somewhere in Nigeria, I noticed in my class that there was a particular set of students that scored low marks always. One day, I made a curious discovery about the life of this set of students. I saw them talking about how they killed some lizards, bought a locally made ring and did some charms to hypnotize women for sex. This kind of involvement leads to foundational problems in the lives of both boys and girls at later years.

HOW DO PEOPLE DEVELOP SICK FOUNDATIONS?

One singular event in a person's life is enough to condition his life forever. Christians should be very careful and know that some things that look harmless on the surface may be the seat of problems. A situation where the mother of a child goes out and another woman breast-feeds the child with her strange breasts, is enough to plant evil spiritual deposits in the life of the child which will lead to sicknesses and all kinds of problems. A family is expecting a male child, having had several female children, but at birth, the newborn turns out to be a female. In disgust, the father shouts, Oh no, not again!" This simple statement will throw the life of the innocent baby into turmoil. She will need serious deliverance later in life from a constant feeling of rejection and disappointment.

Dealing With The Unprofitable Foundation

Satan also uses some hidden things to negatively influence the lives of people. A man who is sponsored to school with stolen money and a student who studies with stolen books will graduate all the same, but their certificates will not prosper them. Whatever they do will amount to nothing because they have deprived some other people directly or indirectly. For God to bless this sort of people, repentance is compulsory because God can never build on a rotten foundation. John 3:27 says, **"A man receives nothing, except it be given him from heaven."** However, some people are impatient with God and seek things from beneath. If you have received things from satan's store house, you must return it before God can work in your life since those strange things would have contaminated your foundation.

Many lives have been contaminated by evil covenants, bad spiritual deposits or some other strange involvement. Naming a person after the dead is a clever demonic way of planting the problem of that dead person into the foundation of the person. This is the reason believers who understand the activities of demons and spiritual warfare do not give their children names like Babatunde (the dead father has come back), Iyabo (the dead mother has come back), Nneka (mother is supreme) and similar names that affirm reincarnation of the dead. It is a culture of Babylon.

Laying on of hands is a very important biblical doctrine for appointment into office, blessing, receiving Holy Spirit or healing the sick. But if a demonic person lays hands upon you, it is a disaster because demonic powers could flow into you just as the power of

Dealing With The Unprofitable Foundation

God could flow into you when it is done by a true minister of God.

Signs of a sick foundation:
1. Persistent emotional problems.
2. Hatred.
3. Anger.
4. Fear.
5. Self-pity.
6. Depression.
7. Uncontrollable crave for evil things.
8. Sore tongue.
9. Misuse of God's gifts.
10. Hearing strange voices.
11. Inability to receive the Holy Spirit baptism.
12. Involvement in religious errors (vegetarianism, celibacy, etc).
13. Absolute confidence in drugs.
14. Inability to have a steady home.
15. Suicidal tendency.
16. Feeling caged.

Many people have got used to poverty, failure and other problems because these things have long been in their lives. These problems came in as a result of some doors which were opened by the individuals concerned or doors opened by their parents. There is good news in spite of all these. A sick foundation does not mean the end of life. You can repair your foundation if you so desire. Hezekiah means the strength of Jehovah and he tapped it to the fullest. You too can do that today if only you care. King Hezekiah, who turned out to be one of the best kings in Israel, had a sick foundation because his father was highly demonic. 2 Chronicles 28:1-2 says,

"Ahaz was twenty years old when he began to reign, and he reigned sixteen years in Jerusalem: but he did not that which was right in the sight of the Lord, like David his father; for he walked in the ways of the kings of Israel, and made molten images for Baalim. Verse 4 says, "He sacrificed also and burnt incense in the high places, and on the hills, and under every green tree."

Today, many people are foolishly following the evil paths of their fathers. Sometime ago, when I was counselling one old woman, she told me that she could not change her religion even though she had realised that the religion could not give life. Her excuse was that her husband was already dead and that was the religion of the family. To her, it would amount to betrayal if she accepted Jesus Christ. This kind of person will move from one confusion to another until she accepts Christ who is Lord of all. We thank God that King Hezekiah made the wise choice.

"And Hezekiah sent to all Israel and Judah, and wrote letters also to Ephraim and Manasseh, that they should come to the house of the Lord at Jerusalem, to keep the Passover unto the Lord God of Israel. So he established a decree to make proclamation throughout all Israel, from

Beersheba even to Dan, that they should come to keep the Passover unto the Lord God of Israel at Jerusalem: for they had not done it for a long time in such sort as it was written." (2 Chronicles 30:1, 5)

King Hezekiah had a desire to break away from his sick foundation and he took concrete steps to ensure that it was done. Unfortunately today, many people seek for deliverance just by mere words of mouth. Recently, a lady troubled by water spirit and spirit of fornication was being counselled and right there she was making passes at someone. She had to attend to one strange man before she agreed to pray. Part of what she said was that she had undergone series of deliverance in the past to no avail. This kind of lady has a sick foundation and until it is healed, she will remain a failure. She needs to take concrete steps and be sincere.

Hezekiah knew what he wanted and he went for it. 2 Kings 18:4 says, *"He removed the high places and brake the images, and cut down the groves, and brake in pieces the brazen serpent that Moses had made: for until those days the children of Israel did burn incense to it: and he called it Nehushtan."* He knew his father had laid a terrible foundation so he opted for another one. You do not have to inherit a bad foundation. You can say no today. Galatians 3:13 says, *"Christ hath redeemed us from the curse of the law, being made a curse for us; for it is written, cursed is everyone that hangeth on a tree."* And Colossians 2:14 says, *"Blotting out the handwriting of ordinances that was against us, which was contrary to us, and took it out of the way, nailing it to his cross."*

This is what Jesus Christ has done for us as the great architect and builder of all ages. If you already have a sick foundation, tap the power in Jesus Christ as King Hezekiah did and you will never be the same again. Many would have died many years ago, but they are still living. Many, who were poor, are now living in abundance. Many broken homes have been mended and are now enjoying marital bliss. Those who were almost destroyed are now preaching the gospel of salvation. Believe God to cure your sick foundation and He will do it. He can never, and has never failed.

Chapter Two

PULLING DOWN
FOUNDATIONAL JERICHO

Dealing With The Unprofitable Foundation

This chapter is talking about three things. The first one is a "Pulling down" exercise, then there is "Foundational", and then there is a "Jericho." We will analyze these three things one after the other. First, we will look at Jericho. Readers of the Bible who have read the book of Joshua will recognize that Jericho was a stronghold hindering the Israelites from entering the promised land. There was a promised land to enter, but before the children of Israel could go into the land flowing with milk and honey, they had to pass through a well fortified city known as Jericho. The place took a lot of spiritual bombardment and Holy Ghost fireworks before it fell. God asked them to march around the place for 7 days. You may ask, "Did God not have power to point to Jericho and make it fall in just one second?" If yes, why did not He just do that? He did not do it, because He wanted to teach His people the principles of warfare. God instructed them to go round the wall for seven days and on the seventh day when the priests sound the trumpet, they should all shout. They did as God had instructed them, and the wall of Jericho came crumbling down. Some Bible scholars tell us that the more appropriate way to describe the incident is that the wall sank. The falling of this wall made way for the children of Israel and they were able to enter the promised land. The journey of the Israelites can be compared to our own journey as Christians. Many of us have personal Jerichos and you may be passing through your own now. You will have to pull it down. Psalm 78:2, *"I will open my mouth in a parable: I will utter dark sayings of old."* This means that some sayings are dark.

Dealing With The Unprofitable Foundation

The Bible is the most wonderful book in the world, and no book can beat it. It stands in the middle of creation, for it tells us about the past, the present and the future. Although it was written by about 40 men who never met themselves within a time frame of about 1,000 years, yet one can see the coherence in what they wrote. The Bible is the only book that will stand when all other things are gone. There are many questions in the Bible. To some, answers are provided, e.g. *"Has the Lord delight in burnt offering and sacrifices than hearkening to his voice?"* To this an answer is provided; *"Behold, obedience is better than sacrifice."* Another one is, *"is there no balm in Gilead or no physician? Why is it that the health of the daughters of my people is not restored?"* To this there is no answer. In Psalm 8 verse 4, another question is asked, *"What is man, that thou art mindful of him? And the son of man that thou visitest him?"* to this also, there is no answer.

There is also another question; *"Is any sick among you?"* This one has an answer: *"Let him call for the elders of the church, let them pray for him and anoint him with oil."* Jesus asked another question, "When the son of man shall come, will he find faith on earth?" This one has no answer. Many questions in the Bible are quite challenging, and they need serious consideration. Let us look at a very important question which will lead us to various things. This question can be found in Psalm 11:3. No answer was supplied to this question. It says, *"If the foundations be destroyed, what can the righteous do?"* This question takes us to the analysis of the second aspect of our topic, Foundation.

Dealing With The Unprofitable Foundation

WHAT IS FOUNDATION?

If you want to make the foundation of a building, you will dig holes in the earth and lay the foundation there. The foundation that makes buildings stand is usually hidden and ugly. It suffers the most, and it is the one that carries the whole weight of the building. Foundation blocks are usually buried in the dark at the base of the building. While it is possible to see the fine building, the foundation is hidden in the dark, where it cannot be checked after the building has been completed. It is possible for some parts of a building to be changed or replaced e.g. windows, doors, etc. But if the foundation is bad, nothing can be done about it. Another thing is that a foundation cannot be altered neither can it be repaired. The foundation is hidden deeply beneath a building. No one can see it, yet it accomplished the task. All other blocks and structure on top of the foundation need it to be able to stand.

Beloved, the foundation of a person's life is just like any other foundation we have described. In anything we do, whether physically or spiritually, there must be a foundation. The Bible says, even the church of God is built on the foundation of the apostles. It is the foundation that will determine whether a building will be stable and durable. It will determine the type of building and the purpose for which it can be used. For anything we do or intend to do, the foundation is very important. For example, the reason many marriages collapse is bad foundation.

Dealing With The Unprofitable Foundation

Sometime ago, when I was in England, a friend asked me to escort him to the airport to welcome his wife. I obliged him and followed him. When we got to the airport, to my amazement, he put his hand into his pocket and brought out a picture. And as people were arriving, he kept looking at the picture and at their faces. I was embarrassed because we were both PhD students in England. I had to ask him to confirm if he did not know the lady we came to welcome. He told me that his parents arranged the wedding in absentia and that they have only posted the wife to him. He stayed there searching, and then suddenly a light complexioned lady arrived. He looked at her, called her name, the lady too called his name and they then embraced each other. That was how they got married at the airport! I was therefore not surprised two years after, when the Nigerian girl, who was about 23 years old, ran off with a white German who was 60 years old. My friend wanted to commit suicide but I advised him to take it easy. I also told him that if he died, the girl would continue to enjoy herself. The problem of that marriage was due to bad foundation.

When a marriage is not based on love and the will of God, but on lust, it has a bad foundation. When a marriage is based on accidental pregnancy, and the couple were forced to marry as a result of the pregnancy, such a marriage would end up a failure as it was built on bad foundation. When a marriage is based on beauty, handsomeness and other physical features like long legs, long hands, etc, such a marriage has a bad foundation. When a marriage is based on the fact that the would-be husband has money, then the foundation is bad. Unfortunately for many sisters, many of the nice brothers do not have money. When a woman marries a man because of money, the man will certainly treat the wife like an object. Not being born again before getting married is bad foundation because the choice of husband or wife would be made randomly out of various men or women. These are some of the reasons why marriages collapse.

If you find a marriage that is about to collapse, the first thing to check out is how it all started, that is the foundation. Was it strong and solid? Or was it done because two influential families compulsorily joined them together. One of the most foolish things any builder can do is to build a house without foundation or use a bad foundation. We can therefore assume that where there is no foundation, there is no building or where there is poor foundation; there will also be a poor building. I remember the story of those two men who wanted to build. One built on the rock (strong foundation), while the other built on sand. When the winds came and the storm blew on the two of them, with the same strength and current, while the building on the sand collapsed and great was its ruin, the one on the rock stood firm. The Bible says that, "Many are the afflictions of the righteous, but the Lord delivereth him from them all." However, any affliction that starts from the foundation of a person's life needs very serious action because:

1. The foundation cannot be seen.
2. The person has now grown above the foundation.
3. The beautiful nature of the external structure will not tell you what is at the foundation.

So, the instability of many lives today is due to their faulty foundation. Ninety percent of stubborn problems brought to the house of God is due to faulty foundations. I'll like to share this testimony with you. At the church I was long time ago, something happened. There was a herbalist living around the church with two wives. Suddenly, one of the wives started to fellowship with us at our church. The woman heard the message and realized that it was wrong remaining married to the herbalist. So, she decided not to marry the herbalist again. The herbalist did not like this. He came to the church and told us to tell his wife to leave our church. We told him that we had no right to stop anyone from coming to church. He then threatened that he would use his evil means. He ended up running away from the area.

There was another incident of a woman who was pregnant, and was attending herbal antenatal clinic. They agreed that on the day of her delivery, she would pay three hundred naira. The day she fell into labour, she could not afford the money. She was rushed to the herbalist, who insisted on having the money before starting anything. They were able to raise half of the money after running around so much. The man then began the process of taking delivery of the baby. He started to rain his incantation and the woman gave birth to the first baby of the twins. The herbalist now requested for the balance of the money before taking delivery of the second baby. They ran around again and got the man the balance. The man tried all he could but the baby did not come out. The woman was in pains and almost at the point of death when the husband came from work.

He decided to take her to her hometown, when he saw her condition. He put her into a taxi and they headed for the woman's hometown. Along the way, somebody who knew the woman saw her and enquired about her problem. When the man was told the woman's story, he invited them to a prayer revival meeting taking place at his church nearby. They put the woman in their centre and before they could say "Father in the name of Jesus," she gave birth to the second baby. Now, there is a problem. One of the woman's babies, Taiye was born in the home of a herbalist and the other, Kehinde was born in the house of God. We cannot expect the course of their lives to be the same because they have different foundation.

Foundational problems are the most difficult problems anyone can think of. Should you destroy a building to get to its foundation? What should you do? This is why the Bible in its wisdom, prohibits so many things which it sometimes does not explain why. When you then begin to understand why God banned these things, you will be surprised.

There is too much wickedness amongst the black race. The first offence that anyone can commit is to be doing well. Some people will say that they have not offended anybody or done anything wrong. You don't need to do anything bad to get them offended. The simple decision by you to do well is enough to get them offended, and they will be after you. These wicked people among the black race do all sorts of wicked things to people. They collect blood from babies and manipulate the blood. This simple collection affects the baby for life. And if this baby does not know the way of the cross, he will go from

Dealing With The Unprofitable Foundation

the cradle to the grave with one problem or the other. People go around clinics, asking for placentas to buy, and once they get them, they can permanently destroy the baby's life through that means. They look for sand underneath people's feet, manipulate the sand and put the people in trouble. They collect fingernails and hairs and use them against people. They give bad concoctions to babies to drink and from that moment, such babies get into trouble. Some people have the foundation of idolatry; they bear names that glorify idols.

Many people were born without familiar spirits, but somebody gave things to them to eat, and they suddenly discovered that they have acquired strange powers. They struggle to get out, but they find it impossible. There is currently a serious mass exercise of initiations in schools. Parents must warn their children not to take things from strangers or things distributed at schools from their mates claiming to be celebrating their birthday. They should be very alert and reject such items. It is dangerous to accept such things because lots of children have been unconsciously initiated this way.

When some people were young, their parents hung charms on their necks and waists. These are avenues of problems. All these foundational things are better known as foundational Jericho. They have to be pulled down. The worst thing about foundational problems is that people were not aware, they did not know, and cannot even tell when they were planted. Some people were raped at very young ages and those demons are still harassing them. In the house where I lived long ago, there were a lot of bachelors there, and there was also one woman there who had twins and used to cook beans every Friday. Most of these young men used to prepare in advance for her beans by buying bread. She never knew that these twins were being put into trouble. What the enemy wanted to spoil in many lives, he had already done at the foundation, at the level or stage when there was little or no consciousness.

Your being born again is a way to get out of these problems. Getting born again is not the solution; it is only a way to the solutions. Unless specific praying is done, the problems will generally remain or try to hide. The Bible says that the habitation of the wicked is full of cruelty. There was a small boy who felt like easing himself at around 2 a.m. one day. As he was going to the toilet, one spirit told him to look through the keyhole of an old woman staying in the same compound, in order to see what she was doing. The small boy went to peep through the key hold and to his amazement, he saw the old woman of about 80 years old, standing naked in the middle of her room as she began to transform to a young girl from the top of her head downwards. She completely transformed to a young girl of about 21 years. After she had dressed up in some lace material she then prepared to go out. The boy was dumbfounded and transfixed at the woman's door, so could not move away until she started opening the door. Although the boy ran away, his eyes had been bewitched.

This is the time for you to do a very serious fight with satan. These prayer points may look strange to new comers in the school of warfare, but they work and bring results. For example what do you understand by the following prayer points?

1. O Lord, send your fire to the foundation of my life, and let it burn to ashes everything presently affecting me in a negative way, in the name of Jesus.
2. I break and loose myself from any bondage that I might have inherited from my parents, in the name of Jesus.
3. O Lord, release me from foundational problems, in the name of Jesus.
4. I refuse to follow any evil design or pattern laid down by my ancestors, in Jesus' name.
5. Holy Ghost fire, destroy the roots of inherited evil plantations, in the name of Jesus.

What do you understand by these prayer points and why do you think we pray them? It is because 90 percent of the problems that are resistant to normal praying are rooted in the foundation. The problem of evil foundation is so enormous that it has completely messed up many lives. When I was in Abuja recently, a sister came for counselling and brought two hospital reports. One of the reports showed that she was five months pregnant while the other one said that there was no trace of a baby in her womb. How do you explain this? The doctors got confused, but by the time we started praying, it was revealed that the problem had to do with her foundation. In her family, they had promised some idols that they will be supplying them a specific number of babies every year and the quota for the year had not been met. So, they removed her baby with plans to remove three more.

Our Lord Jesus Himself understood this and at a point He pointed accusing fingers at the background of the Jews. (Matthew 2:29-35). The Jews are called the generation of those who killed the prophets. For example, some women complained that their husbands don't stay at home and that they always move around with strange women or strange vultures. What we are saying is that this problem may have nothing to do with your husband. It may be from your own foundation. Perhaps, your father was a polygamist, and that spirit has entered into you and you have transferred it to your husband. This is the spirit of polygamy which creates the desire to have many women. Until this is broken, the problem will remain.

You will be deceiving yourself if you choose to dismiss with carelessness, your background or participation in masquerades, tribal rituals, collection of your name from an oracle, being born by a father who has charms, amulets and idols at home, parents who accept services from demons, parents who were harsh to slaves or by parents who pound day old babies to protect themselves, and being born in a polygamous set-up. You will be deceiving yourself to believe that all these will just fly past you without any effect. It is not possible at all. The great truth is that the full scope of evil foundation has not been adequately understood by present day believers.

Dealing With The Unprofitable Foundation

Many are saved, sanctified, and filled with the Holy Ghost, thank God for them. All these are like spiritual soaps for washing the spirit. Until they are used, they would not wash. It is like buying the biggest Bible in the world and wrapping it in the most expensive snake skin case. Until the Holy Ghost fireworks get into the root of our lives, many black Christians will never be free. There was a sister who at 36 years was not menstruating. She was fortunate to hear a message on evil foundation. She first of all sat down and confessed her involvement in ancestral idolatry and rebuked the burdens and bondages of the devil. She then started praying. Note this; when you close your eyes to take a prayer point and begin to say it consistently and violently without allowing your mind to waver, and you concentrate, very soon things will begin to happen positively. However, when you pray sluggishly without concentration, nothing will happen. But when you get aggressive, and you concentrate and spend quality time on prayer points, then you will begin to get results. A person could spend up to 10 hours on just one prayer point to get desired results. The Bible tells us not to make vain repetitions. A vain repetition is when people repeat the same stereotyped, mechanical prayer ceremoniously, day in, day out like parrots. This is the practice in many churches today. The afflicted sister then started praying, "O Lord, send your fire into the root of my life." She prayed the prayer point for one hour, sweating profusely. When you sweat during prayers, the sweat that comes out is healing. After one hour of aggressive praying, faces began to appear. The first face was her grandfather's who appeared with bloody hands in a forest. She did not understand this. Later, she found herself as a small child at the back of her mother, while her mother was fighting with another woman. He mother swore that the child at her back will not prosper, if she did not wound the other woman. Eventually the fight ended and she did not wound the person she fought with. However, she had issued the curse against the poor baby at her back and the curse was then affecting her. Thank God, the aggressive prayers helped the sister.

Sometimes, when we are praying at MFM, it is easy to know the newcomers in the church or those who are old students but have refused to pass our exams. They are not serious with prayers. Sometimes, they open their handbags to get handkerchiefs to wipe away sweat; some switch their head from place to place in an unserious manner as if they are playing with the enemy. The Bible says that, "Right from the time of John the Baptist, the kingdom of God suffereth violence and the violent taketh it by force." Some struggle with their headgears, they do all these unserious things until the bell is jingled and they have not really prayed. These are the strategies of the enemy against these people. We have to be careful and we must take prayer points very seriously with holy madness and aggression, if we are to get desired results.

Do you hear voices that others cannot hear? Do you hear disturbing voices? Are there some thoughts pushing you where you do not want to go? Do you have problems attending Church, reading the Bible, or hearing the preacher or praying? If you do, it then shows that there is something at the foundation that needs to be attacked. What I am saying has nothing to do with whether you were born in a mission house where pastors had been living for long. It has nothing to do with whether they brought you forward for baptism and sanctification on the 40th day, or not. Do you have pains that moves round different parts of your body? Do people threaten you in your dreams? Is your sex life abnormal in any way? Is your life getting harder and your problems getting greater now that you are born again, whereas before you became born again there seemed to be no problem? This means there are some things at the foundation that does not want you to serve God and be in Jesus' camp. Do you see or sense dark figures or smell unpleasant things?

Are you the type of person that goes into uncontrollable anger? If you have anger in your life, it is terrible. This is because anger is the greatest door opener to other evil spirits. It will keep opening doors to evil spirit. Do you ever experience cold presence at night when you sleep? Do you faint? Do you experience continuous nightmares? Do you find it hard to control your thoughts or anger? If you have any of these problems, you need to send fire to your root today and gain your freedom. All these evil background that have been mentioned can lead to spiritual blindness, lack of progress in everything, thoughts of suicide, marital problems, strange accidents, violent deaths, health problems, or serious sexual problems, You can get out of this situation today. It depends on you and what you decide to do with your life.

Dealing With The Unprofitable Foundation

There was a man who came for prayers. He just found out that at 34 that he had not achieved anything and nothing was working for him. He still had to depend on his younger ones for sustenance. If he was given money to start a business, it would not work. He was either duped or something terrible would happen. When we started praying, the spirit of God revealed the secret of his problem and it was a shock to everybody. It was discovered that he was not the real child of his father. The Spirit instructed his mother who was always following him to church to reveal to him who his real true father was. The woman then confessed that, the man was actually the son of her husband's friend. He did not know that until he was 34. He had been relating to the wrong person as his father. Every money the fake father spent on him never yielded good results. When some parents attempt to dictate the sex of their children, they give birth to half men and half women. Some go to local herbalists to achieve this. Going to the herbalist, mark the beginning of another round of problems because evil designs will be put into the lives of those who do that and the problem will go from age to age.

How can we arrest these situations of foundational problems?

The first thing is to know that God is not a failure neither did He create failures. Therefore, no creation of His should be a failure. Every problem of man was finished when Jesus said it was finished on the cross. Whether you want to apply it now, is another thing.

STEPS TO BE TAKEN

1. Identify the source of the problem. This should be done by prayer. God will reveal things to you, if you pray aggressively.
2. Have intense and perfect hatred for the enemy that opened the door of your life.
3. Renounce and reject it out loud. Don't be polite to the devil. Command him to leave in Jesus' name. He will leave only if you harass him to do so.
4. Break all former satanic associations. These include wrong friends, wrong churches, wrong literature, etc.
5. Fill the vacuum with the power of the Holy Spirit.

Only God can go to the foundation and repair it without destroying the building. You have to pray to Him seriously with total concentration, and aggression in your spirit. Before praying, ensure that you are born again, as this is the only way your prayers can be answered. If you are not born again, confess and repent of your sins now and ask the Lord Jesus to come into your life.

PRAYER POINTS

1. *(Place your right hand on your stomach, close to your navel while praying this prayer point)* I drink the blood of Jesus and swallow the fire of the Holy Spirit, in the name of Jesus.

2. Lord Jesus, send your fire to the root of my life, in the name of Jesus.
3. Lord Jesus, release me from foundational problems, in the name of Jesus.
4. Let the fire of God, destroy all my pictures kept in the demonic world, in the name of Jesus.
5. I loose myself from every evil foundational bondage, in the name of Jesus.
6. I severe every problem link between me and my parents, in the name of Jesus.
7. Every placental bondage in my life, be broken now, in the name of Jesus.
8. Father Lord, I command all my buried virtues to be exhumed now, in the name of Jesus.
9. Every dead bone in my life, receive life now, in the name of Jesus.
10. Father Lord, anoint me to be victorious in every area of my life, in the name of Jesus.

Chapter Three

EATERS OF FLESH AND DRINKERS OF BLOOD

Dealing With The Unprofitable Foundation

"When the wicked, even mine enemies and my foes, came upon me to eat my flesh, they stumble and fell." (Psalm 27:2)

The devil is not a fair fighter, he often exploits man's ignorance. No wonder the scripture laments that my people are dying because of lack of knowledge. That a man touches a live wire accidentally does not prevent a shock. So also a person's lack of knowledge about the activities of eaters of flesh and drinkers of blood is inconsequential and does not prevent him from being a victim. This chapter, through the power of the Holy Spirit, would expose to you what eaters of flesh and drinkers of blood are, and how they affect lives. More than this, you would be opportuned to know what to do when they come against you as a flood.

Man is a triune, that is, a spirit living in a body and having a soul. The Bible says, the body without the soul is dead. The body therefore, is like a container housing the spirit. Once the eaters of flesh commence their evil activity in any life, the spirit of the victim is affected accordingly. This is the reason a hungry man cannot be active spiritually. Anything that affects the container will in turn affect the spirit within the container. Evil spirits can live in any part of the human body and have power to put a life in bondage until a superior power challenges them.

The scripture tells us of the encounter Jesus had with a woman held in bondage by the spirit of infirmity for eighteen years. If left unchallenged, they can put a person in bondage from the womb till such a person gets into the grave. There are three different levels of bondage that satan unleashes on his victims:

1. **Demonic Possession:** This is a state where demonic spirits take complete control of a person and use the person at will and even speak through him. Such a person would be speaking more languages than he can when he is in his normal senses. Mark 1:23-25, gives us an example of a man possessed with demonic spirit that was challenged by the presence of Jesus Christ.

    "And there was in their synagogue a man with an unclean spirit; and he cried out saying, let us alone; what have we to do with Thee, thou Jesus of Nazareth? Art thou come to destroy us? And Jesus rebuked him, saying hold thy peace, and come out of him."

    No true Christian who has genuine baptism of the Holy Spirit with the evidence of speaking in tongues can be demon possessed. This is one of the reasons I encourage believers to receive the baptism of the Holy Spirit. John 7:37-38 says, *"In the last day, that great day of the feast, Jesus stood and cried saying, if any man thirst, let him come unto me, and drink. He that believeth on me, as the scripture hath said out of his belly shall flow rivers of living water."*

2. **Demonic Oppression:** This is a situation whereby satan torments and afflicts an individual to make him uncomfortable in life. People have often complained of strange objects moving in their bodies, yet these objects cannot be detected by the X-ray machine. Frequent nightmares and similar horrible experiences are as a result of demonic oppression.

3. **Demonic Obsession:** This is mainly a demonic influence on a person. The victim does not have demons dwelling inside of him but is constantly being harassed.

OPERATIONS

All the forms of demonic activities described above confirm that there are powers that cannot be seen with the physical eyes. Yet, they have considerable influence on the life of man. Once a particular part of a person's body has been eaten up in the spirit world, that organ cannot function anymore, although it may appear alright in the physical. This explains why people are taken to the hospital after serious complaint of pains in some parts of the body, yet the doctors would not be able to diagnose any ailment.

One day, a woman brought her son who looked pale and lifeless to a deliverance meeting. She complained that she had taken the child to numerous hospitals in Nigeria and England but all to no avail. The man of God then prayed for the sick child and God revealed that the sickness was due to the activities of eaters of flesh and drinkers of blood. The shocking aspect of it was that she was part of the eaters of flesh and drinkers of blood troubling her son. In the course of conducting deliverance for this woman, she confessed being a member of a demonic cult where human flesh and blood are taken regularly. Part of her confession was that the liver of her son had been eaten in the spirit world. Little wonder the scripture explains thus: *"Have respect unto the covenant: for the dark places of the earth are full of the habitations of cruelty."* (Psalm 74:20)

The demonic world is full of researchers that are daily exploring new ways of eating up people, whilst they are still living. The reason you find an adult pulling off his hair with his hands although he finds it painful. It is because the hair has been eaten up in the spirit world. When a person has used all medications for stomach discomfort or ulcer and yet there is no cure, it could be that his intestines have been consumed by the eaters of flesh. In Africa, demonic powers manifest through what is known as familiar spirits. They are called familiar spirits because they live among men and carefully familiarize themselves with them so much that it takes the Spirit of God to discern them. Familiar spirits can possess human beings and even animals.

These spirits can obtain information about the past, present and a little into the future about a person. All herbalists, chief priests, fetish people, mystic centres work with familiar spirits. Familiar spirits have powers to appear in various forms. They can even impersonate a dead person. In some parts of the world, when a person dies and those in the family suspect that the person was killed by someone else, they consult a necromancer to inquire who killed the person. The necromancer calls out the supposed spirit of the dead, which in actual fact is a familiar spirit and not the spirit of the dead person. Hebrew 9:27 says, *"And it is appointed unto man once to die, but after this, the judgement."* Anything contrary to this is a lie of the devil. It is the habit of some so-called believers to visit cemeteries during Easter Mondays. They explain that they are doing it after the order of Mary and the disciples who went to look for where Jesus Christ was buried. But the Bible says in Luke 24:5, *"Why seek ye the living among the dead?"*

I went for a funeral one day and on my way out, I saw some young boys and girls in a queue going to pray at some tombs. These young lads may be genuinely ignorant of the implications of such demonic act but ignorance does not absolve them from suffering the repercussion. All such activities are controlled by familiar spirits and will definitely take their toll on participants. If you have ever been involved in such demonic practice, you must seek deliverance. Involvement in all forms of magical art is a direct invitation to familiar spirits. Praying in the names of angels e.g. holy Michael, holy Gabriel, holy Raphael and daily involvement in horoscope are ways of submitting one's life to eaters of flesh. Colossians 2:18 says, *"Let no man beguile you of your reward in a voluntary humility and worshiping of angels, intruding into those things which he hath not seen, vainly puffed up by is flesh."*

"Ye shall not eat anything with the blood neither shall ye use enchantment, nor observe times." (Leviticus 19:26)

Some seemingly innocent actions put people in bondage. For example, visiting diviners or fake prophets, using strange perfumes supposedly to ward off evil spirits, listening to music not inspired by the power of the Holy Spirit such as Rock, Reggae, Fuji and Juju music, watching pornographic films or reading pornographic books are all express journey into bondage and open invitation to eaters of flesh.

For the activities of eaters of flesh to prosper in a life, they must go through the idol worshipped in that particular family whether in the past or at present. A witch from without can only affect a person with the consent of the witch within the family. This is the reason the scripture says: *"For the son dishonoureth the father, the daughter riseth up against her mother, the daughter in law against her mother in-law, a man's enemies are the men of his own household."* (Micah 7:6) I have seen people spend all their earnings on charms and many have travelled thousands of kilometres to consult diviners solely because they live in fear and therefore require protective charms. You may wonder how come these charms work whereas, the Bible says all powers belong to Jesus. Satan has some limited powers and that is the reason he will continue to have followers. But it is a big gamble. When a man relies on a particular charm and that charm comes in contact with another charm energized by a more powerful demonic spirit, the first charm becomes powerless. Herein lies the foolishness of trusting in man, because no matter how powerful a charm is, there will always be a stronger one somewhere. Even more dangerous is the fact that the secret of this charm may be discovered by your opponent one day and it will result in outright defeat.

"Thus saith the Lord; cursed be the man that trusteth in man, and maketh flesh his arm whose heart departeth from the Lord." (Jeremiah 17:5) We thank God that we know that charms can be nullified and the power of our prayers cannot be overcome by the powers of darkness. As part of their activities in the demonic world, these demon powers cause accidents and stir up strife and wars when their blood bank is low.

They also have an infirmity store where deadly sicknesses and diseases are kept. Poverty, dumbness, depression and even diseases that have not been seen on planet earth are in the demonic stores in the second heaven, which is the abode of satan. Persons possessed by this evil spirit are often addicted to tobacco and kolanut, hence you always find herbalists with these things.

A Young man went to his home town and as he was leaving, he distributed money to all those around leaving out only one small girl. This possessed girl that was not given anything started drinking the young man's blood. She agreed to stop tormenting this young man only after she had been appeased with tobacco and kolanut. Meanwhile, she still afflicted the man with the spirit of gambling.

Dealing With The Unprofitable Foundation

Know this fact, no matter how close a possessed person is to you, when it is time to afflict you, he will not show any mercy. No matter how nice you are, a person possessed with the spirit of witchcraft will show no pity. This is why the Bible says, **"Thou shalt not suffer a witch to live."** (Exodus 22:18) Appeasing evil spirits is not a solution.

Victims of eaters of flesh have been asked by demonic advisers to buy fruits, salt or even fry bean cakes (akara) to appease these spirits, but all to no avail. The Bible says: **"Let favour be showed to the wicked, yet will he not learn righteousness: in the land of uprightness will he deal unjustly, and will not behold the majesty of the Lord."** (Isaiah 26:10)

Jesus Christ never appeased any possessed person or spirit. Trying to appease evil spirits is like entering into another courtship with a satanic agent. All evil spirits must be cast away in Jesus' name.

Another wickedness in the demonic world is invocation. The life size statute of a person to be attacked is carved an evil spirits are then invoked into the image which in turn results to emotional torment for the person. At times, this image may be put into fire or pepper could be rubbed on it. This results to high blood pressure in the victim or uncomfortable burning sensations all over his body. A nail or pin could be put into the chest of the image leading to heart-attack or heart-failure. Worse still, there have been cases when such image is cut and tied with a wrapper, put into a coffin and the spirit of death is invoked upon it and buried. The result of this is instant death.

Dealing With The Unprofitable Foundation

Inspite of all these terrible things which confirm that the world is truly the habitation of cruelty, we thank God that none of these demonic things can prosper in the life of a spirit-filled believer. For a church goer or a Christian that still commits sins, there is danger. Many years ago, at a place called Akure in Nigeria, two women had a misunderstanding and one told the other that she would teach her that some women are more equal than others. And the second day, this woman who was forty five years old started bed-wetting. What happened? Eaters of flesh ate her bladder and her system became uncontrollable. She was eventually cured in the name of Jesus at a revival in Akure and she gave her testimony in the presence of thousands of people.

Those in the demonic world use their powers to manipulate the lives of men. Cases have been reported of old men that were at the verge of death only for another younger person to die in their stead thereby fulfilling in a negative way what Isaiah 43:4 says, *"Since thou wast precious in my sight, thou that been honourable, and I have loved thee; therefore will I give men for thee, and people for they life."* Sometimes, in some parts of the world, you would hear or read in the papers that a person is dead only for you to discover after some days that the death story is a hoax. Such a thing has spiritual implications. And more often than not, it is those close to such people with this evil power that die as a replacement.

Dealing With The Unprofitable Foundation

DRINKERS OF BLOOD

Closely related to eaters of flesh, are drinkers of blood. Blood is a very important thing and that is why through the ages, blood had been used for sacrifice. Even the blood of animals is important. *"For it is the life of all flesh; the blood of it is for the life thereof; therefore I said unto the children of Israel, Ye shall eat the blood of no manner of flesh; for the life of all flesh is the blood thereof; whosoever eateth it shall be cut off."* (Leviticus 17:14)

It may sound strange, but the truth is that some powers feed on human blood defying God's warning. People have confessed to drinking men's blood and using it to fry bean-cakes at road-sides. Once the drinkers of blood are in operation in a life, the victim becomes constantly sick and suffers loss of weight. Anyone whose blood is taken by demonic powers will automatically have a short life span.

One of the easiest ways of opening the door of a life to drinkers of blood is by incision. *"Ye are the children of the Lord your God; Ye shall not cut yourselves, nor make any baldness between your eyes for the dead."* (Deut. 14:1)

People go for incisions on their bodies to flee from the bondage of satan. But they forget that darkness can not fight darkness. All forms of incisions are administered by satanic agents. Every form of incision you put on any part of your body has a two-fold implication:

a. You submit your blood to the devil for spiritual manipulation at will through the opening that has been made on your body.
b. You form a blood covenant. The Bible says your life is in your blood. Therefore, each incision signifies the sealing of a blood covenant. Can you afford to be in agreement with satan? You need to break all the blood covenants you have made with the devil if you desire to enjoy an everlasting covenant with God.

An atheist was sick and at the point of death in a teaching hospital somewhere in Nigeria. One of his colleagues visited him and promised to call again in two days time. But this visitor was dumbfounded at the response of his sick colleague who said, "I fear that you may not meet me when next you call because parts of my body are being shared right now. Can't you see?" And that very night, he died. What was the problem? A medically minded person would say that the man was in a state of hallucination while saying those words. But the truth of the matter was that eaters of flesh and drinkers of blood were feasting on him. He knew a little bit too late.

Another secret you should know is that drinkers of blood can drink the blood out of a lovely marriage and it will end up in violent separation. The blood of a good business could be sucked and such business would go bankrupt.

WAY OUT

We thank God that He did not leave us at the mercy of eaters of flesh and drinkers of blood. Isaiah 49:26 says, *"And I will feed them that oppress thee with their own flesh; and they shall be drunken with their own blood, as with sweet wine; and all flesh shall know that I the Lord am thy saviour and thy Redeemer, the mighty One of Jacob."*

This is the sure promise of God and it can never fail. If the Holy Spirit is convicting you that you are a victim of eaters of flesh and drinkers of blood, you need to prayerfully command all eaters of flesh to vomit every organ of yours that has been eaten and also command all drinkers of blood to vomit your blood that they have taken, in the name of Jesus. The Bible says, *"He hath swallowed down riches, and he shall vomit them up again: God shall cast them out of his belly."* (Job 20:15) This is the stand of God and satan can not go against it the moment he realises that you have discovered your rights.

A final thing you will have to do is to issue another strong command energized by the power of the Holy Spirit to force all eaters of flesh to begin to eat their own flesh and every drinker of blood to drink their own blood. Then command every organ in your body to begin to function correctly. *"For by him were all things created that are in heaven, and that are in the earth, visible and invisible, whether they be thrones, or dominions or principalities or powers; all things were created by him and for him. And he is before all things, and by him all things consist."* (Col. 1:16-17)

Chapter Four
THE POWERS THAT PURSUE

Dealing With The Unprofitable Foundation

"And if the avenger of blood pursue after him, then they shall not deliver the slayer up into his hands; because he smote his neighbour unwittingly, and hated him not beforetime." (Joshua 20:5)

"Life is not a resting, but a moving," says one anonymous writer. If it just stops at that, there would not be any cause for alarm. But life is more than just a moving. Some people in the course of this moving have moved into lifelong problems unconsciously. A wrong step taken at any point could result in an injury that would be nursed forever. Eccl. 9:12 says, *"For man knoweth not his time; as the fishes that are taken in an evil net, and as the birds are caught in the snare; so are the sons of men snared in an evil time, when it falleth suddenly upon them."* The worst problem a man can have is when he is chased about by powers that are bent on destroying him. In the course of this hot chase, the person being pursued could be wounded, if not caught. Worse still, he could loose his life in the process. A life could be pursued from cradle to the grave. This is the case with individuals with chain problems who never experience lasting peace till they die.

A young man was admitted for typhoid fever at a hospital a few years ago. The doctor in charge gave specific instructions that he should not be injected with a particular drug. When it was time for drugs to be given to him, he reminded the nurse on duty that the doctor had instructed that he should not take a particular drug. The nurse nodded in agreement as the information was already on the bedside card. In spite of all these precautions, the nurse still injected this young man with the wrong drug. There was serious commotion in the whole of the hospital that day but God intervened and the young man did not die. How does one explain this sort of case? The truth of the matter is that this young man was being pursued by some powers and these powers even pursued him to the hospital.

A person wakes up very early in the morning and carries sacrifice to a road junction in a university community. Another one goes to the bar beach to take a special bath at unholy hours. Someone builds a house and each time he sleeps, he hears some strange sounds. A woman ties charms on the waist of her child and refuses to remove it. An individual runs from one diviner to another, and an educated person with all the degrees in this world hears some strange voices (each time he is alone) urging him to commit suicide. All these people have one thing in common. Their lives are under hot pursuit and until the right thing is done, peace will continue to elude them.

WHAT ARE THE POWERS THAT PURSUE MAN?

1. **VENGEANCE**
    Anything a person does in life must be rewarded whether good or bad. This is the reason the scripture says: *"Be not deceived; God is not mocked; for whatsoever a man soweth, that shall he also reap."* (Galatians 6:7) *"And I will execute great vengeance upon them with furious rebukes; and they shall know that I am the*

Lord, when I shall lay my vengeance upon them." (Ezekiel 25:17) God is the ultimate rewarder of deeds. It is a great pity that many lives are under the hammer of God's vengeance today. Somebody was talking to me one day about how he went into a harlot and later discovered that he had contacted venereal disease. Instead of seeking for cure, he took a decision to sleep with many harlots in that particular hotel so as to ensure that all of them contacted this disease. Whilst he was relating this experience to me, it was as if something was pounding inside my head. At the end of his story, I told him a Bible truth that vengeance will catch up with him one day, unless he repents and seek for forgiveness. If you have wrongly taken anything from another person, you must take corrective measure or else you will subject your life to pursuit by vengeance. A lady in her prime was collecting money and gifts from different men. When she was ready to marry, she picked one and told herself that life was win some loose some. By this action, she already qualified for the hammer of vengeance. One of the reasons God refuses to bless some people despite all the praying they do is because their lives are pursued by vengeance.

A brother heard the gospel, got converted and heard the message which says, *"He that steals should steal no more."* He decided to return all the things he had stolen from his place of work. But on his way to return those things, he met devil's counsellor who told him that such an act was fanatical and stupid. He had already had an unforgettable encounter with

Dealing With The Unprofitable Foundation

God the great provider, so he did not go back. Those little things you pilfer from your office, as little as they seem, may be responsible for your falling victim to robbers and fraudster every time. You are an unmarried Christian, but the tax form you fill at the beginning of every year, says that you are married with four children. Vengeance will cry. People who subject others to unnecessary tests and trials will have God's vengeance crying upon them. I was at a restaurant some years ago. Two men sat opposite my table and were discussing how each of them will test the sincerity of their wives by making illicit advances to each other's wife. These two men will be judged by God's vengeance for subjecting their innocent wives to unnecessary trials.

The wickedness in the demonic world is so intense that God said that the vengeance He will visit on the wicked ones will be carried over to their children.

"The Lord is long suffering, and of great mercy forgiving iniquity and transgression, and by no means clearing the guilty, visiting the iniquity of the fathers upon the children unto the third and fourth generations." (Numbers 14:18)

There have been reports of places where day old babies are used for money-making charms. Will God continue to look? He would not. In 1964, I was at a Pentecostal church somewhere in

Nigeria. All of a sudden the pastor ran from the front to the main entrance at the back of the church. Meanwhile, a woman had just entered and was clapping her hands. The pastor shouted at the woman, "Turn over!" In response the woman said, "Yes sir," and walked to her seat. Much later, when I began to discern spiritual things, I understood that short drama between the pastor and the woman. Whilst the woman was walking with her two legs in the physical, in the spirit realm, she was actually walking into the church on her head, the reason the pastor told her to turn over. This woman will definitely be visited by God's vengeance for allowing herself to be used by satan to disturb the work of God. Each time you cause unnecessary troubles in your local assembly, you are inviting God's anger. The scripture says, *"It is a fearful thing to fall into the hands of the living God."* (Heb. 10:31)

What to do once you realise you are under torment as a result of God's vengeance

The Jews know what vengeance is all about and they understand that there must be a payback. This is the reason they told Apostle Paul at the island of Melita that he must be a murderer, although he was not. *"And when the barbarians saw the venomous beast hang on his hand, they said among themselves, No doubt this man is a murderer, whom, though he hath escaped the sea, yet vengeance suffereth not to live."* (Acts 28:4)

A person that is being pursued by God's vengeance cannot experience the peace of God. No herbalist, priest or prophet can bail the person out except he takes the prescription of God.

"Repent ye therefore and be converted, that your sins may be blotted out, when the time of refreshing shall come from the presence of the Lord." (Acts 3:19)

The next thing you must do is restitution, no matter how shameful or uncomfortable it seems. It is better to be ridiculed momentarily than for one to experience eternal damnation. As you take these steps you shall be freed in Jesus' name.

2. **CRYING BLOOD**

Many innocent blood is shed daily and God will never overlook such iniquity. Like I mentioned in the previous chapters, the Bible says, the life of the flesh is in the blood, so shedding blood in any form for whatever reason is a serious issue as far as God is concerned. As the blood of Abel cried unto God for revenge, so is the blood of every innocent person shed today crying to God for vengeance. The Jews, because they are a special breed of people understand that blood cannot be shed in vain. This is why at the crucifixion of our Lord Jesus Christ, they shouted: *"His blood be upon us, and our children."* (Matthew 27:25) And that is what is happening even till this day. The blood of all the saints that are killed will cry for revenge and God will hearken to such cries because he has already forbidden shedding of blood.

"Whoso sheddeth man's blood, by man shall his blood be shed; for in the image of God made He man." (Genesis 9:6)

There are four groups of people that shed blood and they will pay for it unless they repent genuinely:

i. All those that reject the blood that Jesus Christ shed at Calvary. The scripture calls them offenders. Careless Christians that do not believe that the atonement provided in the blood of Jesus Christ suffices for everything should be warned. People, who are still involved in one form of sacrifice or the other, are guilty of trampling upon the precious blood of Jesus Christ.

ii. Those that have in any way been involved in committing abortion. The law of your country may say it is right but the word of God says it is wrong. Therefore, if you do not want to be pursued by blood, you will abide by God's word.

"Also in thy skirts is found the blood of the souls of the poor innocents; I have not found it by secret search, but upon all these." (Jeremiah 2:34) That you committed an abortion with the consent of your husband does not make you guiltless, because in the process, you might have killed God's ministers.

iii. Those that take Holy Communion unworthily. Christians who have lost sight of the importance of Holy Communion may be inviting the powers that pursue upon themselves. You keep malice, fornicate, tell lies and live a sinful life daily, yet you gladly receive Holy Communion on Sunday. I am sorry to inform you that you have embarked on a very dangerous journey.

Wherefore, whosoever shall eat this bread, and drink this cup of the Lord unworthily shall be guilty of the body and blood of the Lord. But let every man examine himself, and so let him eat of that bread, and drink of that cup. For he that eateth and drinketh unworthily, eateth and drinketh damnation to himself, not discerning the Lord's body." (I Corinthians 11:27-29)

iv. Haters of the brethren. Any root of hatred inside you against a fellow brother or sister makes you qualify to be pursued. It may appear a simple thing but Christians must not take it lightly because it is part of the reasons Jesus Christ said that God will reject the offering and sacrifice of some people.

(Whosoever hateth his brother is a murderer; and you know that no murderer hath eternal life abiding in him." (I John 3:15) God will always seek to avenge all innocent blood that is shed, particularly the blood of saints. *"Therefore as I live saith the Lord God, I will prepare thee unto blood, and blood shall pursue thee: seeth thou hast not hated blood, even blood shall pursue thee."* (Ezekiel 35:6) It is the blood that many have shed in the past that is now tormenting them today.

Way out: Repent seriously, pray specifically about all the blood you have shed and tell God to forgive you. He will do it and you will have a respite.

3. **SIN**

   John 5 tells us about the encounter Jesus Christ had with a man that sin caught up with and kept in bondage for 38 years. After healing him, Jesus gave him a warning: *"Behold, thou art made whole: sin no more, lest a worse thing come unto thee."* (John 5:14)

   Sin is a strong power that pursues people and no matter where you run to, your sin will definitely find you out. A story is told of a boy who saw something like a puppy and took it home. He carefully kept it away from his parents by making an abode for it in the roof and the puppy was growing there. One day, he forgot to feed it and the animal had to come down from the roof. Behold, it was a young lion. It devoured everyone in that family. That is exactly the way sin is. People, without realizing the gravity of what they do, feed sin regularly until the day it becomes an unmanageable monster.

As a Christian, if you go to cinema houses to watch films not inspired by the Holy Spirit, you are feeding sin. I know a gentleman who smokes only in his bedroom. He seemed to be a clever smoker. But what does the Bible says?

"Though hand join in hand, the wicked shall not be unpunished: but the seed of the righteous shall be delivered." (Proverbs 11:21)

God does not play with sin and as for Him, there is no small or big sin. Whilst some receive instant punishment for their sins, God allows the cup of iniquity of others to become full before visiting them. Today, the devil in his craftiness has encouraged some careless Christians to rebuild that which the power of God had already destroyed in their lives. Now we have Christian disco, Holy Ghost Jazz, spiritual reggae and funky Christianity. People that need to be delivered from the spirit of lust now embrace people of the opposite sex with the excuse of kissing one another with an holy kiss. Whereas, the Bible admonishes us to abstain from every appearance of evil. *"For if I build again the things which I destroyed, I make myself a transgressor."* (Galatians 2:18) God can not be mocked. Rather than being stylish about committing sin, seek for deliverance from whatever spirit is controlling you. As you take this step, sin will not pursue you again.

4. ENEMY

The scripture defines another class of pursuers as the enemies. *"Israel hath cast off the thing that is good: the enemy shall pursue him."* (Hosea 8:3) Enemies have pursued and killed many more people than war or disease in this part of the world. No wonder the Bible warns us about household enemies. *"For the son dishonoureth the father, the daughter riseth up against her mother, the daughter in law against her mother in law; a man's enemies are the men of his own house."* (Micah 7:6)

Life is a continuous battle. People have had terrible attacks in their dreams only to wake up with paralysis. To others, such attacks have led to instant death after a few minutes of struggle. Ephesians 6:12 says, *"For we wrestle not against flesh and blood, but against principalities, against powers, against the rulers of darkness of this world, against spiritual wickedness in high places."*

When a person is being pursued by enemies, what should be done?

Take solace in the unfailing arm of Jesus Christ. Get filled with the power of the Holy Spirit which is the power from the third heaven. No other power can prevail over the power of God. As you do this, your confession shall be as the Psalmist: ***"Blessed be the Lord my strength, which teacheth my hands to war, and my fingers to fight."*** (Psalm 144:1)

5. STRANGE COVENANT

Strange covenants entered into directly or indirectly can pursue a person's life until death. Some people's lives have been contaminated from birth, while others were donated to idols at tender ages. Except all these demonic contracts are broken, such lives will be under constant pursuit. A lady who had a standing covenant with familiar spirits gained admission into a university. On campus, she joined a gospel group and was fellowshipping with them forgetting about the covenant. One night, members of her cult came and issued her a threat of failure. She said she had Jesus, yet that covenant remained in place. Eventually, she failed all her papers in the final exam. Why? She was being pursued because of a covenant she had not broken. Jesus did not prevent her failure because she had actually not surrendered everything. She got relief only after a man of God conducted deliverance for her. Then she graduated and has been free ever since. You must confess all the strange covenants operating in your life and break them in Jesus' name.

6. **YOUR BEHAVIOUR**

Your behaviour is capable of bringing goodness or problems into your life without anybody cursing or blessing you. Some people have done things that have placed their lives under permanent pursuit. A woman was advising me one day that as a minister, I must see myself as a dustbin. What she said was correct. However, those that behave to me as if they are actually dealing with a dustbin will be bringing their lives into self bondage. A couple that always quarrel with each other will be exposing their children to demonic attacks. A man that gambles will be sending out an invitation to the spirit of poverty by his life style. You must take deliberate steps to give your life to Jesus Christ.

"Therefore, if a man be in Christ, he is a new creature: Old things are passed away; behold, all things are become new." (2 Corinthians 5:17)

Unserious Christians who say that the spirit is willing but the flesh is weak will only extend their stay in the bondage of satan.

7. CURSES

Many people are being pursued by curses. Some are even under curses they know nothing about and these curses are pursuing them.

"Moreover all these curses shall come upon thee, and shall pursue thee, and overtake thee, till thou be destroyed." (Deuteronomy 28:45)

Christians should be mindful of the things they do and how far they relate with people opposed to Christ. There are some things that place people automatically under curses. Just as a person can inherit good treasures, so also can one inherit curses as in the case of Gehazi (2 Kings 5:26-27) A man that attended one of our revival meetings sometime ago, complained of a devastated and confused life. In the course of prayer, God revealed a woman who was pulling his neck. The man later confessed that the woman used to be his first wife but he divorced her and married another woman. He confessed to have broken the marriage vow between him and his first wife thereby placing himself under a curse.

The best remedy for this situation is found in the name of Jesus Christ. Special bath at a flowing river, reciting some incantations and similar demonic methods cannot work. Darkness cannot fight darkness, that is an infallible law. The

Bible says: **"Christ hath redeemed us from the curse of the law..."**

No matter which of these seven powers is pursuing you, there is a city of refuge where security is certain. This city is in the name of Jesus Christ.

A woman testified at one of our meetings how the enemies started pursuing her immediately she got married. They threatened that she would not have the fruit of the womb. Each time she attended a crusade or visited a man of God for counselling and prayers, these powers will visit her in the dream to reaffirm their threat. After some years, she became pregnant but these powers did not give up the pursuit. She was told that she was not carrying a child and that she would give birth to a wood. On the day of delivery, these evil pursuers wanted to take her life when they realized that they had failed. But thank God who has every power in heaven and on earth. This woman gave birth to a bouncing baby. There are numerous cases like this. What power is pursuing you? You too can boldly say like the Psalmist:

"Our soul is escaped as a bird out of the snare of the fowlers; the snare is broken, and we are escaped. Our help is in the name of the LORD, who made heaven and earth." (Psalm 124:7-8)

Decide to escape into freedom today.

Chapter Five

THE UNPROFITABLE COVENANT

Dealing With The Unprofitable Foundation

"And your covenant with death shall be disannulled, and your agreement with hell shall not stand." (Isaiah 28:18)

Two young people stood before a priest in the full view of a large congregation. The priest read a series of passages from the Bible and each of the couple replied; "I do." That is it. A covenant has been sealed. To break it is to invite problems.

A covenant is a strong and binding agreement between two parties. It is similar to a contract with specific terms of operation. There are many forms of covenant, but all of them have one thing in common. A covenant cannot just be broken at the wish of any of the partners.

God can make a covenant with man and when the terms of such a covenant are kept, you can be sure that the benefits would be innumerable.

"And when Abram was ninety years and nine, the Lord appeared to Abram, and said unto him, I am the Almighty God; walk before me, and be thou perfect. And I will make my covenant between me and thee, and will multiply thee exceedingly."
"Neither shall thy name any more be called Abram, but thy name shall be Abraham; for a father of many nations have I made thee."
"And I will give unto thee, and to thy seed after thee, the land wherein thou art a stranger, all the land of Canaan, for an everlasting possession; and I will be their God."

"This is my covenant, which thou shall keep between me and you, and thy seed after thee; Every man child among you shall be circumcised." (Gen. 17:1-2, 5, 8, 10)

This is an example of God entering into a covenant with a man. In this covenant, the terms are spelt out, its benefits and the token of the covenant. Up till this day, the covenant is still binding and that is the main reason the nation called Israel can never be defeated. No other singular nation has been persecuted and threatened with extermination as Israel. Yet, because there was a covenant made, Israel still stands out. God still respects this covenant. I believe you now appreciate how strong a covenant is. Two men can enter into a covenant and anything that is agreed upon becomes binding. A marriage between two people is a covenant and God frowns at any betrayal. God is against divorce and separation. Single parenthood is a curse and anything that works against the marriage institution is contrary to God's will.

"What therefore God hath joined together, let not man put asunder." (Matthew 19:6) One of the easiest ways people bring themselves under a curse is by breaching their marriage vows. If you have been unfaithful to your partner, you must repent today and cry unto the Lord for forgiveness.

Strange though, yet it is a truth that over the years, many have entered into strange covenants with the devil. The devil promises to give men temporary benefits in return for their souls. Unaware of the grave consequences, many have fallen prey to this bait. A man seeking power to excel goes to sleep at a cemetery for twenty-one days. He gets power but loses his soul in exchange. I have seen many people seeking deliverance and making strange confessions. A lady once said: "I have promised to die on my wedding day." To this kind of case, if nothing concrete is done, this person will die because she was only repeating a covenant. Another dangerous aspect of forming a covenant with the devil is that a participant may not be conscious of the involvement, yet it is binding. You can be brought under the power and influence of a contrary covenant by proxy. A pregnant woman makes a covenant with the village idol that the child she bears will serve that idol all his life. Although the baby did not enter into the covenant himself, yet, the agreement the mother made would be binding on him. Many unsettled lives today are as a result of this kind of covenant. This is the reason believers really need to probe into their past and that of their parents. That you have now accepted Christ does not automatically annul this covenant. You must specifically pray and break it.

"If they shall confess their iniquity, and the iniquity of their fathers, with trespass which they have trespassed against me, and that also they have walked contrary unto me. Then will I remember my covenant with Jacob, and also my covenant with Isaac, and also my covenant with Abraham will I remember; and I will remember the land." (Leviticus 26:40, 42)

Dealing With The Unprofitable Foundation

The most dangerous form of covenant is a covenant between man and demonic forces. This is one of the reasons cruelty thrives in the land and people are under a seemingly unbreakable bondage.

WHY GOD ALLOWS THE DEVIL TO THRIVE

The first reason God allows satan to thrive is to prove men. Satan's test serves as examination for us. Without those trials, we would be boasting of what we are not capable of doing. If a man says he has overcome hot temper, not until he maintains his cool in the face of serious provocation, he can never be said to have overcome the spirit of anger. A second reason is to demonstrate God's power over the devil. The intervention of God's power to calm storms has proved to men that there is a power greater than all the powers of hell put together. Thirdly, the presence of the devil and our ability to withstand and overcome his devices will be the basis of our future reward. You get a reward for each temptation you overcome. You do not wear a crown without winning a battle. Finally, the presence of darkness teaches us lessons, develops our faith and builds our character. It is unfortunate that many seem to learn more and better in times of hardship. When some people were living in plenty, they never found their way into the church. But when the wealth disappeared, they began to seek solace in Jesus Christ. The same Jesus Christ they had refused initially. So, the presence of the devil is God's wisdom. The only way to be free from satan is to die. As long as you live, life becomes a continuous battlefield. This is the reason

Dealing With The Unprofitable Foundation

Jesus told His own, *"Lo, I am with you always till the end of the world."* (Matt. 28:20)

Instead of man to rest on the eternal promise of God that cannot fail, many have sought succour from the devil. Some got into covenant with the devil while looking for protection in life's fierce battle ground, some in the pursuit of fame, money, position, power of even children. Each visit a man pays to a herbalist or a diviner is step into bondage. These people are like ambassadors representing the kingdom of satan. Any agreement with them is an agreement with the devil, no matter how mild it may look on the surface. Every form of incision is a blood covenant with satan. That you have received the baptism of the Holy Spirit does not nullify the covenant, you have to specifically break it. Young men and women who ignorantly order for magical books from the East are binding themselves into an unprofitable covenant. If you have ever sought for healing from a traditional healer, you have tattoo on your body or you have been told by your parents that they dedicated you before an idol on the eight day of your birth, you have a covenant to break. Some simple things like reading some Psalms at a particular and in a particular position, burning candles of different colours and keeping the wax at a corner inside your house, makes one to enter into a covenant that may affect not only you, but your whole family.

One day, a lady that had some covenants to break suddenly claimed that she was delivered because she attended a church where she was given fourteen strokes of the cane. This is just a clever device of satan to keep his victims under permanent lock. The scripture says in the name of Jesus, shall evil spirits submit and unprofitable covenants broken. Not by beating or any other form of sacrifice.

"That at the name of Jesus every knee should bow, of things in heaven and things in earth and under the earth." (Philippians 2:10) The name of Jesus Christ still suffices for all situations. What unprofitable covenant have you entered into? What kind of covenant did you inherit at birth? For you to be delivered totally, you need to pray for the Holy Spirit to reveal to you every secret in your life.

It is not uncommon these days to hear people confess of having spirit husbands, spirit wives and spirit children. To such people, having children in the physical world becomes a problem and even when they do eventually, it is a transfer of the demon powers. As long as unprofitable covenant exists in any form in your life, you cannot live according to the fullness of God. This is why every born again Christian must really search his life. If in spite of your new birth, you still have strange encounters in your dream and living is still a big problem for you, you have a covenant that is turning down your spirit and that unprofitable covenant must be broken. Jesus Christ is ready to do it for you, if only you will call on Him.

Chapter Six

TABLE OF THE LORD AND TABLE OF THE DEVIL

Dealing With The Unprofitable Foundation

"Ye cannot drink the cup of the Lord, and the cup of devils; Ye cannot be partakers of the Lord's table, and the table of devils." (I Corinthians 10:21)

Food is very vital to existence and one of the easiest ways you can get a man into problem is through food. The very first problem of man came about through food. Human beings can do anything because of food, and this, most of the time has been the cause of numerous problems. God forbade the eating of a certain fruit in the garden of Eden, but man disobeyed.

"And he said, who told thee that thou wast naked? Hast thou eaten of the tree, whereof I commanded thee that thou should not eat?" (Genesis 3:11)

This shows what man can do. Most of the problems of man today, are as a result of a particular food that was taken at a time either physically or spiritually. You may be surprised to discover that the Lord has His own table on which His children feed. It is wonderful experience to feed from God's table. *"They shall enter into my sanctuary, and they shall come near to my table, to minister unto me and they shall keep my charge."* (Ezekiel 44:16)

"Thou preparest a table before me in the presence of mine enemies; thou anointest my head with oil; my cup runneth over." (Psalm 23:5)

The Most high prepares table for some people regularly to make them have their fill. But I am afraid to reveal to you that the devil also organizes food for people regularly. The crux of this message is therefore the need for you to know on whose table you are feeding. Jesus Christ gave an example of the food from the Lord's table when he spoke to the Samaritan woman by the well in Sychar, Samaria. *"But whosoever drinketh of the water that I shall give him shall never thirst, but the water that I shall give him shall be in him a well of water springing up into everlasting life."* (John 4:14) When you drink from the Lord's table, you will never thirst again, and when you eat from His table, you will not fall sick. Healing for the spirit and body is one of the food items present on the Lord's table. It is sad to realise that many people instead of beholding the food, they are carried away by side attractions masterminded by satan through the enemies of God. That is why the Psalmist said, "In the presence of my enemies." Today's table is being prepared by God in the presence of the enemies because demonic people live together with us, yet, they see us prosper and live in the fullness of God. However, we give thanks to the Lord for a table He will prepare in future. There will be no single enemy around then, for all of them will be languishing in hell fire at that time. This is at the marriage supper of the lamb. It is real, and I pray that you will be there, in Jesus' name.

The word of God is another food on the table of the Lord. This is the reason the Psalmist exclaimed: *"How sweet are thy words unto my taste! Yea, sweeter than honey to my mouth!"* (Psalm 119:103) As God feeds His own children with His word, satan also feeds people with his own words. When Jesus Christ came to this world, He did not need to search for the truth because He was truth personified. He did not need to acquire knowledge from anywhere for He was complete wisdom, He needed not to pray for forgiveness because he knew no sin. Jesus Christ was, and remains the master all through. No wonder a song writer presents Jesus thus: "My soul doth magnify the Lord. My spirit praise His name. For death could not hold Him captive, even in the grave, Jesus is Lord." This is the person preparing a table for us. And no demonic power can touch His table. The worst the devil can do is to divert your attention away. He does this by harassing you so that you will lose focus. Satan torments people at the point of their need so that they will be confused and leave God's table. Whatever anyone eats from the devil's table will bring discomfort. Many people fed regularly from the devil's table. Some do it deliberately while others do it innocently. But you must know this, whether you do it consciously or unconsciously, you must pay for it. The devil feeds his guests with slow or fast poison. Some demonic meals have immediate reaction while some may take four, fifteen or even twenty years to manifest.

Every sacrifice, be it at crossroads or distributed from house to house, is dedicated to demons. Today's crossroads are corruption of the cross of Christ used to replace Christ's sacrifice by demonic powers. You would be astonished to discover that sacrifices and similar abominations date back to Bible times: *"For the king of Babylon stood at the parting of the way, at the head of the two ways, to use divination: he made his arrows bright, he consulted with images, he looked in the liver."* (Ezekiel 21:21)

How do you recognise that you have been feeding from the table of the devil?

Anyone who has ever carried sacrifice to anywhere is guilty. Attending places where demonic tongues are spoken and fake prophets operate, visiting herbalists, eating in the dream, involvement in occult practice are all food from satan's table. As a believer, reading or listening to horoscope is feeding from satan's table.

A lady came to me one day and informed me that she had some serious problems and ended up taking fish with some concoction at one herbal home. At the end of the whole episode, the problem did not subside. I told her, "We don't have fish to give you, but we have the name of Jesus." That fish was a food from the table of the devil. What are the things you have eaten from herbalists? Those things must come out of you. You must vomit all the concoction you have swallowed. I do pity children from polygamous families because almost all of them would have been fed from the devil's table at one time or another. If nothing, at least in the course of their mothers seeking protection for them. A lady told me of how she went to a so called spiritual home and prayers had to be said for her with an egg which she had to rub all over her body. This is nothing but feeding from the devil's table.

Dealing With The Unprofitable Foundation

Are you a believer and yet you are being pursued in your dreams by some things? Are you experiencing a certain problem in your life that appears resistant to prayer and fasting? Have you received the Holy Spirit without your situation improving visibly? If this is your situation, you might have fed from the devil's table a long time ago. Perhaps, when you were even a baby and that evil deposit is still inside you. The devil will always chase you until you get rid of his property. As a Christian, you must not be caught up in the web of fashion. You must be sure that the Bible supports everything you do, or else you might be treading on dangerous ground. A believer buys a car and agrees to use alcohol for prayer. He pours libation at his house-warming ceremony. At his child naming ceremony, he agrees to use honey, sugar, dead rats, alligator pepper and similar demonic materials. Such involvement is akin to feeding at the table of the devil. As a believer, your life must be devoid of all forms of heathen practice. You should not pour libation, fry akara (bean cake) to mark any forty days anniversary or shave your head for the dead. All these are open invitation to demonic powers. If that is the tradition in your place, now that you are a believer, your life must be directed by the word of God and not the traditions of men.

"The children gather wood, and the fathers kindle the fire, and the women knead their dough, to make cakes to the queen of heaven, and to pour out drink offerings unto other gods, that they may provoke me to anger." (Jeremiah 7:18)

Devil's food is always cheap. It could hide in a life for many years without the person knowing until the appointed time. No microscope can detect it. A certain woman was force fed in her dream when she was a spinster and from that day her menstruation ceased. Later, she got married and became born again. The Lord stepped into her situation and she got pregnant and got delivered without menstruation contrary to medical science. But before this feat could be achieved, she had to vomit the food she ate from the devil's table. I know of people that have taken such food and it turned to something else in their stomachs. A man took kolanut and it turned into a finger. I had a personal experience some years ago. Someone gave me cake as a present. God told me to keep this cake and not to eat it. The result was unbelievable. After about six months, the cake turned to wood! Two months later, the person who gave me the cake confessed somewhere else of her demonic escapades.

For you to have a breakthrough, you must be prepared to vomit all the things you have eaten from devil's table. You have to challenge those strange things walking round your body with the fire of God. As you do this, you will receive great deliverance in your soul, body and spirit. No matter at what point the food was taken, Jesus Christ had been set up for that purpose:

"How God anointed Jesus of Nazareth with Holy Ghost and with power: who went about doing good, and healing all that were oppressed of the devil: for God was with him." (Acts 10:38)

Dealing With The Unprofitable Foundation

You need to ask God to empower you to vomit all the strange food you have taken from the table of the devil. Furthermore, you need power to refuse to eat in the dream from today. Jesus Christ is more than able to set you free.

Chapter Seven
THE POWER IN THE BLOOD OF JESUS

"And they overcame him by the blood of the Lamb, and by the word of their testimony and they loved not their lives unto the death." (Revelation 12:11)

GOD'S MYSTERIES

God in His infinite wisdom created many mysterious things. Of all these numerous things, there are three of them that are so essential to daily living. They are water, spirit and blood. The scripture says: *"And there are three that bear witness in earth, the spirit, and the water, and the blood; and these three agree in one"*. (I John 5:8)

For any believer to be an effective spiritual warrior, he must continually attack the enemy's stronghold. For you to do this, you must understand the weapons available from God. It is a lie of satan to assume that if you leave the devil alone, he will leave you alone. God expects you to persistently bombard the enemy. If you are going to just be defending yourself, you will lose the battle. If you will ever make spiritual progress, you must carry the warfare right into the camp of the enemy. Any believer that still trembles at the sight of darkness must have his claim to salvation cross-checked. It is our duty to establish the kingdom of God on earth and to attack any force that will not allow the kingdom to be established and set them in disarray. This is the reason the Bible says we are more than conquerors. A conqueror will win, but someone who is more than conqueror will not only win, but will take captive. We are an army of conquerors and the blood of Jesus Christ is a powerful weapon provided for us.

"For the life of the flesh is in the blood; and I have given it to you upon the altar to make an atonement for your souls: for it is the blood that maketh an atonement for the soul. Therefore, I said unto the children of Israel, No soul of you shall eat blood, neither shall any stranger that sojourneth among you eat blood". (Leviticus 17:11-12) Blood is not just any other thing, the reason God places so much emphasis on it. God spoke virtually everything into being, but when it came to man, He brought into display His creative ability by using His own hand to create man. No wonder the Psalmist said, *"I will praise thee: for I am fearfully and wonderfully made."* (Psalm 13:9-14)

Man is a spirit, has a soul and lives in the body. The life in the blood was imparted when God breathed into the nostril of man. Therefore, spiritually, the life of man is in the blood of man. Blood is so powerful and wonderfully made even the blood of animals have the potency to protect and preserve the life of human beings in the Old Testament days before Jesus Christ came.

Job was a good example of someone making regular sacrifices with the blood of animals to preserve his family. The blood of animals sufficed until Job himself broke the protection by his confession of fear.

"He that diggeth a pit shall fall into it; and whoso breaketh an hedge, a serpent shall bite him". (Eccl. 10:8)

God's eternal principles are forever settled. Once it is broken by man, it attracts automatic punishment. The confession of fear on the part of Job amounted to breaking the hedge of protection which the blood sacrifice was providing for him and his family. Listen to Job: *"For the thing which I greatly feared is come upon me, and that which I was afraid of is come unto me."* (Job 3:25) It was Job himself that nullified the power of the blood he was using. This is the reason every believer must be mindful of the things he confesses with his mouth and even inward thoughts. The blood of ram that the Israelites used in Egypt was enough to shelter them from destruction.

"For the Lord will pass through to smite the Egyptians, and when he seeth the blood upon the lintel, and on the two side posts, the Lord will pass over the door, and will not suffer the destroyer to come in unto your houses to smite you". (Exodus 12:23)

All these are conclusive proof of the power in the blood, even the blood of animal. God gave specific rules about the handling of blood. Ignorance was not an excuse should you go against these regulations. Eating and drinking of blood is forbidden by God.

"But flesh with the life thereof, which is the blood thereof, shall ye not eat". (Genesis 9:4)

"Moreover, ye shall eat no manner of blood, whether it be of fowl or of beast, in any of your dwellings". (Leviticus 7:26)

"But that we write unto them, that they abstain from pollutions of idols, and from fornication, and from things strangled, and from blood". (Acts 15:20)

Any involvement that will result to drinking or shedding of blood is an abomination to God.

"Whoso sheddeth man's blood, by man shall his blood be shed; for in the image of God made he man". (Gen. 9:6)

Due to the power God has put into blood, not only shall anyone pay with his own blood for shedding another person's blood unjustly, the land shall also be polluted. This is the reason there are series of mishaps in a particular locality at times and people seem not to understand. Another discovery in the scriptures is that blood speaks! It can talk. Cain killed Abel his brother and thought that it could be hidden from God. Just as many believers are committing sin secretly, yet they are the ones that are most visible at fellowships. God sees them perfectly well.

"And he (God) said, what hast thou done? The voice of thy brother's blood crieth unto me from the ground". (Genesis 4:10) So the blood of Abel was speaking to God, even from the ground. That is the power in the blood.

Dealing With The Unprofitable Foundation

"And they cried with a loud voice, saying, How long, O Lord, holy and true, dost thou not judge and avenge our blood on them that dwell on the earth? And white robes were given unto every one of them: and it was said unto them, that they should rest. Yet for a little season, until their fellow servants also and their brethren that should be killed as they were, should be fulfilled". (Revelation 6:10-11)

Till this day, the blood of all martyrs that were killed for the gospel of Jesus Christ are still calling on God for vengeance. Jesus Christ made a very remarkable statement in Luke 11:49-51:

"Therefore also said the wisdom of God. I will send them prophets and apostles, and some of them they shall slay and persecute: That the blood of all the prophets, which was shed from the foundation of the world, may be required of this generation. From the blood of Abel unto the blood of Zacharias which perished between the altar and the temple. Verily I say unto you it shall be required of this generation".

God places so much premium on blood that He will always avenge any blood shed unjustly. There are some things expressly stated in the Bible and once you do them, the punishment of God becomes automatic. Shedding innocent blood is one of such things. When you enter into a blood covenant with anybody, no matter who, you are engaging yourself in one of the strongest forms of covenants. Couples who have sucked each other's blood as a way of sealing their relationship, need to seek for deliverance. This is the reason the Bible forbids incision. Acupuncture is also another thing believers must be wary of. If you have ever killed any animal for sacrifice, you must seek for deliverance. Animals must be killed only when they are needed for food. Any other thing that makes you shed the blood of an animal puts you under God's judgement. Sacrifices placed at crossroads are not made unto God but unto demonic powers.

"But this man, after he had offered one sacrifice for sins for ever, sat down on the right hand of God; for by one offering, He hath perfected for ever them that are sanctified". (Hebrew 10:12,14).

Offering blood sacrifice is a universal phenomenon and every tribe in the world realise that there is a particular power in sacrifices made with blood. However, the problem with blood covenant in the Old Testament is that the shed blood does not have power to totally remove sin and free people from the bondage of sin. All that is achieved is that sins are covered. This is the reason such sacrifices have to be repeated often.

A brother gave a testimony of a particular incident in which he was involved when he was in the demonic world. He was assigned with two other people to attack a certain Christian sister with a deadly disease. On their way, they met this particular sister praying with other believers. At the shout of "In the name of Jesus", they became frozen. As the prayer continued and there was another shout, "By the authority of Jesus," there was a serious commotion. As the prayer continued and there was another shout, "By the power in the blood of Jesus, immediately, the charm they were carrying spilled on them which resulted in the death of two of them by the third day. God saved this brother so that he would live to give this testimony of the power in the blood of Jesus.

THE BLOOD OF JESUS

The blood of Jesus is unique and it is the once and for all sacrifice. Whenever those fake and commercial prophets come to you with visions demanding sacrifice, tell them that Jesus Christ has been made a sacrifice for you. The Blood of Jesus is unique because there was no intermixing. He was conceived purely by the Holy Ghost, no contamination. Jesus' blood was pure because God Himself prepared it.

"Wherefore when He cometh into the world, He saith, sacrifice and offering Thou wouldedst not, but a body hast Thou prepared Me". (Hebrew 10:5) *"But with the precious Blood of Christ, as a lamb without blemish and without spot".* (I Peter 1:19)

Since blood carried life, the blood of Jesus Christ carries the eternal life of God. Great wonders and miracles will begin to happen if you can understand the power in the blood of Jesus. Revelation 12:11 tells us that through the blood we are made overcomers:
"And they overcame him by the blood of the Lamb, and by the words of their testimonies; and they loved not their lives unto death".

Since blood speaks, what does the blood of Jesus speak? The scripture tells us the blood of Jesus speaks better things than that blood of Abel. Whilst the blood of Abel was crying for revenge, the blood of Jesus is crying for mercy.

"But ye are come unto mount Sion and unto the city of the living God, and the heavenly Jerusalem, and to an innumerable company of angels, to the general assembly and the church of the first born, which are written in heaven, and to God the Judge of all, and to the spirits of just men made perfect, and to Jesus the mediator of the new covenant, and to the blood of sprinkling, that speaketh better things than that of Abel". (Hebrew 12:22-24)

So the blood of Jesus speaks mercy, peace and deliverance from the powers of darkness.

BENEFITS OF THE BLOOD OF JESUS

Immediately man fell in the garden, God started to make a permanent plan for the redemption of man through a permanent sacrifice. He needed somebody and the person must be a man and his blood must be eternal to make His sacrifice eternal and permanent. This is where the devil made a big mistake, he did not know the plans of God. The devil is not all knowing although he pretends to be.

"But we speak the wisdom of God in a mystery, even the hidden wisdom which God ordained before the world unto our glory. Which none of the princes of this world knew: for had they known it, they would not have crucified the Lord of Glory". (I Corinthians 2:7-8)

The devil and all the host of hell can make mistakes and this is what happened by the crucifixion of Jesus Christ, The devil paid dearly for this mistake. This death and resurrection of Jesus Christ has translated into many things for believers. What are the things we can get from this precious blood of Jesus Christ?

1. **REDEMPTION**
    Since the fall of man, everyone has been placed under God's curse which includes poverty, sickness, torment and death. (Deut. 28) But we thank God for Jesus Christ that has given us right to freedom. Every believer has been redeemed from the curse of the law. *"In whom we have redemption through his blood..."* (Ephesians 1:7)

2. **FORGIVENESS**
    The blood of Jesus that speaks better things has provided forgiveness for all our transgressions; *"In whom we have redemption through his blood, the forgiveness of sins, according to the riches of his grace".* (Ephesians 1:7)

3. CLEANSING

"But if we walk in the light, as he is the light, we have fellowship one with another, and the blood of Jesus Christ his son cleanest us from all sin". (I John 1:7) So we are continually cleansed spiritually by the blood of Jesus.

4. JUSTIFICATION

Justification means acquittal. We are declared not guilty not because we are innocent but because someone has paid the penalty. *"Much more than being now justified by his blood, we shall be saved from wrath through him".* (Rom. 5:9)

5. SANCTIFICATION

We are made holy through the blood of Jesus Christ. We are set apart and are God's property. *"Wherefore Jesus also, that he might sanctify the people with his own blood, suffered without the gate".* (Hebrew 13:12)

6. PEACE

The scripture says; *"And the way of peace have they not known".* (Roman 3:17) Through the eternal blood of Jesus Christ, we have peace with God and peace of God. This is a peace that is beyond the price of diamonds.

"And having made peace through the blood of his cross, by him to reconcile all things unto himself; by him, I say, whether they be things in earth, or things in heaven". (Colossians 1:20)

7. **WASHING FROM SIN**

   While all other forms of blood sacrifice could not wash away sin, the precious blood of Jesus Christ washes away our sins and makes us white as snow. *"And from Jesus Christ, who is the faithful witness, and the first begotten of the dead, and the prince of the kings of the earth. Unto him that loved us, and washed us from our sin in his own blood".*

8. **VICTORY**

   Victory over every principality and power has already been provided for each believer in the blood of Jesus Christ. This victory includes victory over the power of sin and all forms of evil forces. *"And they overcame him by the blood of the lamb, and by the word of their testimony; and they love not their lives unto the death".* (Revelation 12:11)

9. **REMISSION OF SIN**

   "And almost all things are by the law purged with the blood; and without shedding of blood is no remission". (Hebrew 9:22)

10. **CLOSENESS WITH GOD**

    We were all strangers to God, but the blood of Jesus Christ now gives us boldness to enter into God's presence. *"Having therefore, brethren, boldness to enter into the holiest by the blood of Jesus".* (Hebrew 10:19)

3. **CLEANSING**
"*But if we walk in the light, as he is the light, we have fellowship one with another, and the blood of Jesus Christ his son cleanest us from all sin*". (I John 1:7) So we are continually cleansed spiritually by the blood of Jesus.

4. **JUSTIFICATION**
Justification means acquittal. We are declared not guilty not because we are innocent but because someone has paid the penalty. "*Much more than being now justified by his blood, we shall be saved from wrath through him*". (Rom. 5:9)

5. **SANCTIFICATION**
We are made holy through the blood of Jesus Christ. We are set apart and are God's property. "*Wherefore Jesus also, that he might sanctify the people with his own blood, suffered without the gate*". (Hebrew 13:12)

6. **PEACE**
The scripture says; "*And the way of peace have they not known*". (Roman 3:17) Through the eternal blood of Jesus Christ, we have peace with God and peace of God. This is a peace that is beyond the price of diamonds.
"*And having made peace through the blood of his cross, by him to reconcile all things unto himself; by him, I say, whether they be things in earth, or things in heaven*". (Colossians 1:20)

7. **WASHING FROM SIN**

    While all other forms of blood sacrifice could not wash away sin, the precious blood of Jesus Christ washes away our sins and makes us white as snow. *"And from Jesus Christ, who is the faithful witness, and the first begotten of the dead, and the prince of the kings of the earth. Unto him that loved us, and washed us from our sin in his own blood".*

8. **VICTORY**

    Victory over every principality and power has already been provided for each believer in the blood of Jesus Christ. This victory includes victory over the power of sin and all forms of evil forces. *"And they overcame him by the blood of the lamb, and by the word of their testimony; and they love not their lives unto the death".* (Revelation 12:11)

9. **REMISSION OF SIN**

    "And almost all things are by the law purged with the blood; and without shedding of blood is no remission". (Hebrew 9:22)

10. **CLOSENESS WITH GOD**

    We were all strangers to God, but the blood of Jesus Christ now gives us boldness to enter into God's presence. *"Having therefore, brethren, boldness to enter into the holiest by the blood of Jesus".* (Hebrew 10:19)

11. PURE CONSCIENCE

It is the blood of Jesus that purges our conscience from filthiness and makes us want to serve God in truth and holiness. *"How much more shall the blood of Christ, who through the eternal Spirit offered himself without spot to God, purge your conscience from dead works to serve the living God"*. (Hebrews 9:14)

12. NEW COVENANT

The blood of Jesus provides us with a new and better covenant. *"Now the God of Peace, that brought again from the dead our Lord Jesus, that great Shepherd of the sheep, through the blood of the everlasting covenant"*. (Hebrew 13:20)

13. NEW BIRTH

Our sonship was provided for through this same blood of Jesus Christ. *"For as much as ye know that ye were not redeemed with corruptible things, as silver and gold, from your vain conversation received by tradition from your fathers; But with the precious blood of Christ, as of a lamb without blemish and without spot. Being born again, not of corruptible seed, but of incorruptible, by the word of God, which liveth and abideth forever"*. (I Peter 1:18-23)

These are the thirteen wonderful benefits and provisions inherent in the precious blood of Jesus Christ. Jesus Christ had to shed his own blood so that you and I can have all these goodness.

SEVEN-FOLD SHEDING OF THE BLOOD OF JESUS CHRIST

1. **Jesus Christ at Gethsemane**
   "And being in agony as he prayed more earnestly, and his sweat was as it were great drops of blood falling down to the ground". (Luke 22:24)

   This act by our Lord Jesus Christ shows us that praying is not that easy neither is it something for the spiritually unserious. Jesus taught us a lesson in intercessory prayer at Gethsemane.

2. **Jesus Christ disfigured**
   "As many were astonied at thee; his visage was so marred more than any man, and his form more than the sons of men". (Isaiah 52:14)

   The face of Jesus Christ was marred and He bled from His face for you and I. This disfigured face stands for the sins of men.

3. **Jesus Christ beaten with stripes**
   Jesus was scourged many lashes for you and I. *"Then released he Barabas unto them; and when he had scourged Jesus, he delivered him to be crucified".* (Matthew 27:16) The blood that came out of His body as a result of the stripes brought healing for every believer. No wonder the Bible says: *"...And with his stripes we are healed".* (Isaiah 53:5)

4. **Christ wore a crown of thorns**
   "And when they had plaited a crown of thorns, they put it on his head, and a reed in his right hand". (Matthew 27:29) What does this crown of thorns stand for? It stands for the breaking curses and as the blood was oozing out, material and spiritual blessing were being given unto mankind.

5. **Christ nailed to the cross**
   "And when they came to the place which is called Calvary, there they crucified him". (Luke 23:33) The hands and legs of Jesus Christ were nailed to the cross with blood dripping out. What does this stand for? You work with your hands and walk with your legs. This particular aspect of Christ's suffering means Jesus has died for all your work and walk.

6. **Jesus Christ dripped blood on the cross for six hours** *(And when the sixth hour was come, there was darkness over the whole land until the ninth hour. And now when even was come, because it was the preparation, that is, the day before the Sabbath, Joseph of Arimathaea, an honourable counsellor craved the body of Jesus".* (Mark 15:33, 42-43) The six hours Jesus spent dripping blood, represent our six thousand years of history. We are in the last one thousand years expecting the rapture of the saints to take place any minute from today. Have you been washed by this blood? Do you understand the blood of Jesus?

7. **Jesus Christ pierced by the side**
   "But one of the soldiers with a spear pierced his side, and forthwith came there out blood and water". (John 19:34) What is the significance of this piercing by the side? The water that gushed out of Jesus' side stands for physical salvation, whilst the blood that oozed out stands for spiritual salvation. This seven-fold shedding of the blood of Jesus Christ tells us the significance of each suffering that Christ passed through for mankind.

With this, the blood of Jesus spells defeat for the devil. The blood of Jesus paves the way for us to heaven. The blood of Jesus drives demons out of our path: When we pray, the blood of Jesus brings judgement to all stubborn creatures.

The devil does not like people pleading the blood of Jesus. You can apply the blood of Jesus to any part of your body and anytime you do this, the blood begins to speak attack and defeat to every evil spirit in that particular part of your body and you will experience instant relief. Every believer must cultivate the habit of pleading the blood of Jesus on their household before going to bed each night. If this is done faithfully and constantly, the result will be devastating in the kingdom of the devil. If any strange thing is moving inside your body, and you challenge it with the blood of Jesus, it will be located and will depart automatically.

Dealing With The Unprofitable Foundation

I remember the case of a girl of six who had fallen in love with the blood of Jesus and her play song was; "There is power, there is power, there is power in the blood of Jesus." Little did this innocent girl know that she was equipping herself with spiritual dynamite each time she sang this song. One fateful day, her underwear fell into the next compound which happened to be occupied by a herbalist. This herbalist was deluded by his master satan to believe the underwear was a charm sent to harm him. He started to rain incantations on the underwear and each time he tried to touch it, an invisible power will hold back his hands. He was engaged in this battle for hours. However, after some hours, this small girl and her mother came knocking at this man's door to make inquiries whether the underwear fell into his compound. On sighting her underwear on the floor, the young girl ran and picked it up and the herbalist was stupefied. What happened? The young girl's underwear had been insulated by the power in the blood of Jesus. It was therefore untouchable for any evil force. You too can become untouchable if only you know how to use this power in the blood of Jesus. There are many things a lot of believers do not know and it is the strategy of the devil to keep people ignorant. Ignorance and discouragement are the two greatest weapons of the devil against believers.

Now that you know so much about the power in the blood of Jesus, your spirit, soul and body must never be the same again.

Chapter Eight

IMMUNITY AGAINST THE OPPRESSORS

"He revealeth the deep and secret things; he knoweth what is in the darkness, and the light dwelleth with him." (Daniel 2:22)

There is only one person that can qualify for the above description and that is the Almighty God. He knows every secret thing. God is the only one that understands both worlds perfectly and will not make any mistake. This message will reveal to you some of the greatest secrets of freedom from the hands of oppressors, particularly in Africa.

Anything affecting your soul, spirit, body, business or anything belonging to you in a negative way is an oppressor. Anything ruling a person's life in a cruel and hard way, is nothing but an oppressor.

CHARACTERISTICS OF AN OPPRESSOR

1. An oppressor keeps men from serving the true God. However, when an oppressor fails in achieving this, he tries hard to ensure that the individual does not make much spiritual progress.
2. For an oppressor to operate in any life, a door must first be opened for the oppressor to enter. Most people open the doors of their lives by themselves, while others get the door opened by their parents.

Dealing With The Unprofitable Foundation

3. Oppressors vary in power. Sometime ago, a man of God was praying for somebody to be delivered from some evil spirits. After much praying, the Lord opened his spiritual eyes to see that the person he was praying for, was surrounded by some soldiers and a lion. Each time this man of God tries to free this person he was praying for, the lion roared and obstructed him. He then asked God for a solution. God told him he needed greater power. He prayed and fasted and afterwards, he was able to administer deliverance to the man. At deliverance sessions sometimes, you command a demon to depart, and off it goes at once. Yet, some other demons will not depart at just one command. So, demons vary in power.
4. Oppressors thrive in the lives of unhappy people. A sad spirit is a gateway for demon powers to come in and operate. Anyone suffering from depression will have a regular traffic of evil spirits in his life.
5. Oppressors have agents in every family. This is regardless of socio-economic status.
6. Human beings invite oppressors consciously or unconsciously into their lives.

DOORS

Many people, including believers often open the doors of their lives unknowingly to oppressors. A small girl that was raped at a tender age has had the door of her life opened to demon traffic. A person who masturbates has opened a door. When people sacrifice their properties to idols, doors are being opened. Somebody is guilty of an offence, yet he is cursing himself to prove his innocence, a door is being opened. The scripture says, it is wrong to pray in the name of angels or to worship angels in any form. So, any person praying in the name of any angel is opening a door. Satan's agents carry the so called sixth and seventh books of Moses, whereas Moses never wrote any sixth or seventh book. Anyone that engages in reading such books will end up in multiple troubles.

"Know ye not that we shall judge angels? How much more things that pertain to this life". (I Corinthians 6:3)

I visited a friend one day and when I got there, his mother implored me to prevail on one of her children not to read the so called sixth and seventh books of Moses. By the time I met this young man, he had already read enough portions of this demonic book to cause him a long term problem. I discovered later that it was the same book that his elder brother read when he could not get a visa for an Overseas trip. He got the visa eventually, but got some other terrible things along. What happened? A door was opened.

If you are a born again Christian, but you can still recite some incantations you have learnt before you got born again, there is an existing door that you must do something about. Before anything

Dealing With The Unprofitable Foundation

else, you must ask the Holy Spirit to wipe off the incantation from your memory. Or may be, you have helped someone to carry sacrifice on your head to a crossroad or to a river side, it is an open invitation to oppressors. It is not a good thing for you to be borrowing people's clothes to wear. If the owners of the clothes are possessed, demons will be transferred into you also. If ministers of God could transfer anointing through ordinary handkerchief, negative things can also be transferred in similar manner. When a woman looking for child seeks help from a herbalist, a demonic door is opened, not only for her, but also for the unborn child. If you have been involved in any of these things, it is neither the fault of God nor the fault of the devil but yours. Something must be done and very fast too. Many people have been spiritually contaminated. The contamination must be removed.

There are different kinds of marks in the physical. Some could be cleansed easily, while others would take extra efforts and some could remain permanent. This is the reason one hour prayer could solve some problems while some others will remain unshaken in spite of many days of serious prayers.

I remember praying for a lady some years ago and a demon spirit speaking from her mouth said, "Leave me alone, this person has been dedicated to me from birth. Did she tell you she wants to be free?" What was the problem? A door was opened many years ago and the oppressors rushed in. Any life suffering from spiritual contamination will have a chain of problems. God never created

Dealing With The Unprofitable Foundation

broken nerves, lunatics, and people with diverse problems. All these things happen at a later stage in people's lives after their spirits have been contaminated, some even before birth. People dedicate their children to idols and as such, start problems for them early in life. When a so called Christian is harbouring unforgiving spirit or has hot temper, a door is opened. When you depend on horoscope, your life is being opened to oppressors. It is strange to know that many people seek problems for themselves through involvement in things that will end up putting them in bondage. When a Christian cooks and distributes beans weekly on behalf of his twins, a door is opened to oppressors because such things have no biblical backing. Anyone that is involved in anything based on traditions of men and cannot be established expressly in the Bible, is opening a door. Have you stopped to ask yourself the source of your name or what that name means? If the source of your name is questionable, such name must be changed as it has a tendency to keep your life under bondage. Astral travel is demonic and is an easy way for satan to contaminate your spirit. This is the reason people who engage in it behave strangely.

A woman came for one of our meetings some few years ago and narrated a terrible ordeal she went through. Her husband was not showing her enough love, so she resorted to consulting a fake prophet who started making passes at her and gave her different kinds of charms. It was at this point she realized that she was at the wrong camp and that doors to oppressors had been opened. In the course of praying for this woman, God revealed all the things she had done. She confessed and brought the charms prepared by this false prophet. It was after this that she received deliverance.

There is need for you to carry out a detailed inventory of all the things in your home. These items of decorations in your home, what are their sources and what do they symbolize? I have been shocked by some strange behaviours I see around. For example, recently, a woman died and her daughter started kissing her corpse. This is very strange and highly demonic. By this seeming expression of love, demons of death have been transferred into the life of the young lady.

Satan operates like a fly at times. When a fly lays eggs on a particular spot, these eggs may not be seen with the naked eyes immediately, but they are there all the same. The same is true of spiritual eggs. At the time they are laid, they remain unnoticed but when the eggs metamorphose into maggots and flies, then the problems become very visible. Flies lay eggs on fertile soils where the eggs will develop. You must not allow oppressors to move near you. The old saying that prevention is better than cure still holds sway today.

Now that you have been fully exposed to how people open doors consciously and unconsciously to oppressors, it would be advantageous for you to know how you can immune your life from the powers of the oppressors.

Many years ago in Nigeria, there was cholera out-break and instantly the government rose to the challenge by providing the citizens with anti-cholera vaccine. Most of those vaccinated never suffered from the disease. Why? They automatically became immune through the vaccination. You too can enjoy spiritual vaccinations that will immune you from the powers of the oppressors today.

HOW TO BE IMMUNE

1. **LIVE A LIFE OF HOLINESS**

    Things just do not happen all of a sudden, a door is needed. Holy living annoys the devil. Any Christian with a pure heart will be constantly surrounded by the fire of God. Ordinary eyes cannot perceive this fire but satan and his agents can see it. This is one of the reasons demonic agents avoid people that live a holy life. When a believer gets too close with an unbeliever, he makes his life vulnerable to attack by demonic forces. Anyone that confesses to be a Christian and his closest friends are nominal Christians or even unbelievers, such a believer needs deliverance from some strange spirits.

    "Be ye not unequally yoked together with unbelievers; for what fellowship hath righteousness with unrighteousness? And what communion hath light with darkness?" (2 Corinthians 6:14)

Dealing With The Unprofitable Foundation

When you clear your temple of filth and you are continually filled with the power of God, you will be immune. But this is a big task. A lazy Christian can never be holy. Holiness requires your studying the Bible daily and disciplining your body by not allowing your flesh to control you. Holiness demands aggressive prayer life and a constant walk in the spirit.

Do you want to be immune from oppressors? Examine your life carefully and see to it that there is nothing therein that can invite the oppressors. Say no to envy, fighting, malice, hunger and unforgiving spirit.

There was a man that sought the help of a herbalist to harm his friend. Surprisingly, the herbalist asked him if he had fought with his friend, and the man said, "No." The herbalist advised that he must first cause trouble with his friend before any charm would work against him because the man to be attacked happened to be a believer. This shows the power in living a life of holiness.

2. **WALK IN THE SPIRIT**

When you give your life to Christ and you are genuinely baptised in the Holy Spirit, the fire of God will guard you and make your environment too hot for evil powers to thrive.

"This I say then, walk in the Spirit, and ye shall not fulfil the lust of the flesh". (Galatians 5:16)

The Holy Ghost fire brings every strange thoughts into captivity as you walk in the Spirit. When you walk in the Spirit, you pray in tongues always and you ask for guidance from the Holy Spirit before you do anything or take any step. It is a wonderful experience to walk in the Spirit. However, when it is the flesh and human mind that are in control, you have opened the doors for the oppressors.

3. **LIVE A HUMBLE LIFE**

    You must be humble through and through. When you set humility against the devil, he will flee. The humble man occupies a high place in heaven.

    "For thus saith the high and lofty one that inhabiteth eternity, whose name is Holy; I dwell in the high and Holy place, with him also that is of a contrite and humble spirit, to revive the spirit of the humble, and to revive the heart of the contrite ones." (Isaiah 57:15) You must submit yourself totally to the control of God.
    "Humble yourselves therefore under the mighty hand of God, that he may exalt you in due time." (I Peter 5:6).

4. **MEDITATION ON GOD'S WORDS**

    The word of God is the mirror of the spirit for correction unto godliness. For you to permanently shut the doors of your life against oppressors, you need a good dosage of the word of God inside your spirit. The living word of God has the power to transform life.

5. **KEEP THE RIGHT COMPANY**

    For you to be immune against oppressors, you must keep away from all possible sources of contamination. A believer's best friend cannot be an unbeliever. After God has delivered you from a group of alcoholics, you must not go back and fellowship with such group unless you are not sincere. *"Be not deceived; evil communication corrupts good manners."* (I Corinthians 15:33)

6. **FELLOWSHIP WITH THE RIGHT CHURCH**

    You must ensure that you fellowship with a Bible believing and Bible teaching congregation. You must not continue to stay at a particular church just because of any worldly attachment. A Christian that will be immune from oppressors will be one that attends a church that believes in the totality of the word of God, the power in the Holy Ghost and the accompanying gifts.

7. **PUT ON THE WHOLE ARMOUR OF GOD**

    Putting on the whole armour of God demands that you must be truthful in all situations, be righteous and witness your salvation to others. You must involve yourself in things that will develop your faith and you must have an assurance of salvation within your spirit.

"Wherefore take unto you the whole armour of God, that ye may be able to withstand in evil day, and having done all to stand, Stand therefore, having your loins gird about with truth, and having on the breast plate of righteousness." (Ephesians 6:12-13)

8. DISPOSE OFF ALL EVIL MATERIALS

Finally, you must rid your home of all demonic materials so that oppressors will not find a ladder to come into your life.

"Neither shalt thou bring an abomination into thine house, lest thou be a cursed thing like it; but thou shalt utterly detest it, and thou shalt utterly abhor it; for it is a cursed thing." (Deuteronomy 7:26)

Prevention is forever better than cure. The eight principles I have stated above are able to keep the doors of your life shut from the powers of oppressors. It is a wiser thing for you to remain immune against the oppressors than for you too allow your life to be contaminated and start seeking for deliverance. The price is often very high.

Chapter Nine

DECLARE WAR ON SATAN'S WAR

Dealing With The Unprofitable Foundation

"Touch not my anointed and o my prophets no harm." (Psalm 105:15)

As you read this final message, the Holy Spirit will point out your own situation. The Lord speaks no useless words neither does He do anything without a reason. Once God gives you a revelation about a situation, it is like a sound of war, the next thing is to pick up the gauntlet.

Generic praying is a subtle strategy of the devil. A man that has fornicated must confess and specifically name the sin before God and ask for forgiveness. When you say, "Lord forgive all my sins," it is a vain confession. This is the reason a lot of people are still being accused by satan and he continues to prosper in their lives. Some people only need confession and God will forgive them and they will begin to enjoy abundant freedom. Some cases are as simple as that, but the devil is beclouding their vision.

You must declare war against the devil. Not until you do this, he will continue to harass you. And if nothing is done, the purpose of God will not be fulfilled in the individual's life. The exposition in God's words prove beyond any doubt that there is a spiritual battle going on daily. It is either you fight or you are spoiled. These are the only two options and the choice is the personal decision of an individual.

"For we wrestle not against flesh and blood, but against principalities, against powers, against the rulers of the darkness of this world, against

spiritual wickedness in high places. Wherefore take unto you the whole armour of God, that ye may be able to withstand in the evil day and having done all, to stand." (Ephesians 6:12, 13).

"Have respect unto the covenant: for the dark places of the earth are full of habitations of cruelty." (Psalm 74:20)

"He teacheth my hands to war, so that a bow of steel is broken by mine arm." (Psalm 18:34)

"Blessed be the Lord my strength, which teacheth my hands to war, and my finger to fight." (Psalm 144:1)

All these scriptures make us to understand that we are in a battle field and must fight. All those we see in one form of bondage or the other are victims or better still prisoners of war. Is your marriage, finance, health, and children a victim? No matte how fierce the battle you are facing, Jesus Christ came that you should be free if you desire. The thrust of this book is anchored on this passage:

"The Spirit of the Lord is upon me, because he hath anointed me to preach the gospel to the poor; he hath sent me to heal the broken hearted, to preach deliverance to the captives, recovering of sight to the blind, to set at liberty them that are bruised." (St. Luke 4:18)

Dealing With The Unprofitable Foundation

EIGHT PRINCIPLES OF WARFARE

I. You must learn to worship God.
ii. Recognize your enemy by focusing on the spirit behind the problem.
iii. Know your spiritual weapons and how to use them effectively.
iv. Learn how to bind the enemy and loose goodness into your life.
v. Pull down all the contrary strongholds in your life.
vi. Cast down all satanic imaginations propelling your life.
vii. Put all your strange thoughts into captivity.
viii. Be orderly in your warfare; attack one problem at a time.

These eight principles are necessary for your effective deliverance. In earlier chapters, I mentioned that this book is a practical guide towards total freedom and not just a literature for information. You will find below a seven (7) day prayer programme which you should endeavour to do. It is suggested that you do it as a prayer and fasting programme and things will begin to happen, even before the end of the programme.

DAY 1: PURSUE, OVERTAKE AND RECOVER
Scripture Reading: 1 Samuel 30
Confession: Psalm 18:37
1. Thank God for His love, and mercy on you.
2. The Lord should ordain terrifying noises unto the camp of the enemies of the gospel in my life, in the name of Jesus.

3. I command every satanic embargo on my goodness and prosperity to be scattered to irreparable pieces, in Jesus' name.
4. Holy Spirit, set me on fire for God, in the name of Jesus.
5. Every door of attack on my spiritual progress, be closed, in Jesus' name.
6. The thunder fire of God should strike down all demonic strongholds manufactured against me, in the name of Jesus.
7. The Lord should bring too naught every evil counsellor and counsel against me, in the name of Jesus.

DAY 2: KNOW THE SECRET
Scripture Reading: Daniel 2
Confession: Daniel 2:22 & Eph. 1:17
1. Thank God for the Holy Spirit.
2. The Lord should give unto me the spirit of revelation and wisdom in the knowledge of Him, in the name of Jesus.
3. The Lord should remove spiritual cataract from my eyes, in the name of Jesus.
4. Lord, forgive me for every false motive or thought that has ever been formed in my heart since the day I was born till today, in the name of Jesus.
5. The Lord should open up my understanding, in the name of Jesus.
6. The Lord should reveal to me every secret behind any problem that I have, in Jesus' name.

7. Ask the Lord for divine wisdom to operate in your life, in the name of Jesus.

DAY 3: AVENGE ME OF MINE ADVERSARIES
Scripture Reading: Luke 18
Confession: Psalm 18:45-47

1. Praise the Lord because the gates of hell shall not prevail against His Church, in the name of Jesus.
2. Thank the Lord for His promises that are yea and amen, in the name of Jesus.
3. I command every form of demonic family bondage to break, in Jesus' name.
4. I loose myself from the hold and influence of every ancestral spirit, in Jesus' name.
5. I command every bad spiritual deposit to be melted away by the fire of the Holy Ghost, in the name of Jesus.
6. I retrieve my blood or any material from my body from every evil altar, in Jesus' name.
7. I loose myself from every linkage to any family idol, in the name of Jesus.
8. Let every tongue contrary to my peace, be permanently silenced, in Jesus' name.
9. Let every altar of witchcraft, familiar spirits and false religion, be broken in this country, in Jesus' name.

DAY 4: HEAL ME AND SAVE ME
Scripture Reading: Proverbs 4
Confession: Jeremiah 17:14

1. Give thanks as the Holy Spirit leads you.
2. Lord, cleanse me from every filthiness of the spirit, in the name of Jesus.
3. The Lord should promote me from minimum to maximum, in the name of Jesus.
4. Let every evil device against my health be disappointed, in Jesus' name.
5. I reject and denounce every spirit of failure, in the name of Jesus.
6. I overthrow the citadel of sickness, weakness and fear in my life, in Jesus' name.
7. Let me be transfused with the blood of the Lord Jesus Christ, in the name of Jesus.
8. Lord, clothe me with the mantle of fire, in the name of Jesus.
9. Lord, give me the grace to live in divine health, in the name of Jesus.

DAY 5: DEATH TO THE PHARAOHS AND HERODS
Scripture Reading: Exodus 14, Acts 12:21-24
Confession: Isaiah 54:14-15, Jer. 46:17

1. Thank God who daily loads us with benefits, in the name of Jesus.

2. Let all diviners and enchanters hired against me, fall after the order of Balaam, in Jesus' name.
3. Let all my Pharaohs perish in the red sea, in Jesus' name.
4. Let all my Herods be devoured by spiritual worms, in Jesus' name.
5. Lord, fill me to the brim with your power, in the name of Jesus.
6. I command the stronghold of fear, worry and anxiety to be pulled down in my life, in Jesus' name.
7. Let all the drinkers of blood and the eaters of flesh eat their own flesh and drink their own blood, in the name of Jesus.

DAY 6: I DECREE BREAKTHROUGHS
Scripture Reading: Lamentations 3
Confession: Psalm 16:6
1. Thank God for His unfailing love, in the name of Jesus.
2. I bind every spirit of financial failure, in the name of Jesus.
3. Ask for the anointing to prosper, in the name of Jesus.
4. Lord, give me a breakthrough spiritually, financially and martially, in Jesus' name.
5. Let Holy Spirit take perfect control of my tongue, in the name of Jesus.
6. Lord, make this programme the beginning of great tings in my life, in the name of Jesus.
7. I decree that my stolen blessings should be restored seven folds, in the name of Jesus.

DAY 7: LEAD ME TO THE ROCK

Scripture Reading: Mark 9:1-10

Confession: Psalm 61:2-3

1. Thank God for the last lap of this programme, in the name of Jesus.
2. Lord, convert my desert to fruitful land, in the name of Jesus.
3. The Lord should convert my minimum to maximum, in the name of Jesus.
4. The Lord should convert my defeat into victory, in the name of Jesus.
5. Lord, lead me to the rock that is higher than I, in the name of Jesus.
6. I fire back all arrows, enchantments and spells issued against me or any member of my family, in the name of Jesus.
7. Lord, I ask for power and wisdom to run the race set before me, in the name of Jesus.

Other books published by MFM Ministries
- Students In The School Of Fear
- The Vagabond Spirit
- Power Must Change Hands
- Breakthrough Prayers For Business Professionals
- Pray Your Way To Breakthroughs (Third Edition)
- Spiritual Warfare And The Home
- Victory Over Satanic Dreams (Second Edition)
- Personal Spiritual Check-Up
- Prayers That Bring Miracles (In English, Hausa, Igbo & Yoruba Languages)
- Adura Agbayori (Yoruba Version Of The Second Edition Of Pray Your Way To Breakthroughs)
- How To Obtain Personal Deliverance (Second Edition)
- Power Against Local Wickedness
- Brokenness
- Let God Answer By Fire (In English, French, Hausa, Igbo And Yoruba Languages)
- Release From Destructive Covenants.
- Prier Jusquea Remporter La Victoire (French Edition Of Pray Your Way To Breakthroughs)
- Power Against Spiritual Terrorists.
- Deliverance Of The Head
- Revoking Evil Decrees
- The Great Deliverance

- *Wealth Must Change Hands*
- *Limiting God*
- *Power Against Coffin Spirits*
- *Satanic Diversion Of The Black Race*
- *Prayers To Mount Up With Wings As Eagles (In English, French, Hausa, Igbo And Yoruba Languages)*
- *Holy Cry*
- *Power Against Destiny Quenchers*
- *Prayer Rain*
- *Holy Fever*
- *The Fire Of Revival*
- *Be Prepared*

This and other publications of MFM Ministries can be obtained from:

MFM PRESS & BOOKSTORE

54, Akeju Street, Off Shipeolu Street,
Onipanu, Lagos.

MFM BOOKSHOP

13, Olasimbo Street, off Olumo Road,
by Unilag 2nd Gate,
Onike, Yaba, Lagos, Nigeria.
Or any other leading Christian bookstores.

MFM AND THE AUTHOR

Dr.D.K. Olukoya is the General Overseer of the Mountain of Fire and Miracles Ministries and The Battle Cry Christian Ministries.

The Mountain of Fire and Miracles Ministries Headquarters is the largest single Christian congregation in Africa with attendance of over 120,000 in single meetings.

MFM is a full gospel ministry devoted to the revival of Apostolic signs, Holy Ghost Fireworks, miracles and the unlimited demonstration of the power of God to deliver to the uttermost. Absolute holiness within and without as spiritual insecticide and pre-requisite for heaven is openly taught. MFM is a do-it-yourself Gospel Ministry, where your hands are trained to wage war and your fingers to do battles.

Dr. Olukoya holds a first class honours degree in Micro-biology from the University of Lagos and a PhD in Molecular Genetics from the University of Reading, United Kingdom. As a researcher, he has over seventy scientific publications to his credit.

Anointed by God. Dr. Olukoya is a prophet, evangelist, teacher and preacher of the Word. His life and that of his wife, Shade and their son Elijah Toluwani are living proofs that all power belongs to God.

Published by:
The PRESSHOUSE
MOUNTAIN OF FIRE AND MIRACLES MINISTRIES
13,Olasimbo Street, Off Olumo Road (near UNILAG 2nd Gate),Onike.
P. O. Box 2990, Sabo, Tel: 867439, 868766, Lagos. Nigeria.
E-mail: mfm@micro.com.ng mfm@nigol.net.ng Website: www.mountain-of-fire.com

www.ingramcontent.com/pod-product-compliance
Lightning Source LLC
Chambersburg PA
CBHW070949180426
43194CB00041B/1891